THE CHILDREN'S FILM

GENRE, NATION AND NARRATIVE

NOEL BROWN

WALLFLOWER

LONDON and NEW YORK

A Wallflower Press Book
Published by
Columbia University Press
Publishers Since 1893
New York • Chichester, West Sussex
cup.columbia.edu

A complete CIP record is available from the Library of Congress

ISBN 978-0-231-18269-0 (pbk. : alk. paper)
ISBN 978-0-231-85111-4 (e-book)

Columbia University Press books are printed on permanent and durable acid-free paper.

Printed in the United States of America

Cover image: *Emil and the Detectives* (1931) © Universum Film (UFA)

CONTENTS

ACKNOWLEDGEMENTS

Thanks to Yoram Allon, Commissioning Editor at Wallflower Press, for his initial enthusiasm and support of this book along the way, and to everyone at Wallflower Press that has contributed in some way to its completion. To Bruce Babington for his invaluable insights and comments on early versions of the manuscript. And to Alan and Kate Brown, Robin and Helen Brown, and Mauricio Martusceli, with love, for help and support of many kinds.

1   THE CHILDREN'S FILM

This book is concerned with the diverse body of fictional texts produced and received as 'children's films'. It will examine their recurrent themes and ideologies, and common narrative and stylistic principles. It will explore how children's cinema has developed across its broad historical and geographic span, analysing changes and continuities in how it has been conceived. And it will discuss key critical issues, while providing case studies of major children's films from around the world. In short, it aims to introduce readers to a large, but vastly under-addressed, subject of enquiry. There have been substantial case studies of children's cinema in various countries, including the United States (Brown 2012), Britain (Staples 1997; Brown 2016), Germany (Schäfer 2009) and Italy (Boero 2013), as well as many shorter pieces addressing specific movements and cycles. There have also been major works on individual studios, such as Disney, and studies of genres and media closely associated with children's cinema, such as fantasy, fairy tale and animation. What has been lacking is a single volume that presents an overview of films for children in their historical and cultural diversity.

Children's films are objects of pleasure, fascination and nostalgia for audiences of all ages, and their appeal cuts across boundaries of class, race, sex, language, culture and nation. The form encompasses feature films and short films, silent films and sound films, live-action and animated films, and various combinations of the above. Few forms of cinema polarise opinion in quite the same way, or mean so many different things to different people at different stages in life. However, relatively few critics have addressed children's films as serious texts. Even fewer have attempted to define what they are, and what they are not. This opening chapter, which is divided into three sections, brings this question into sharper focus. First, it offers a detailed response to the deceptively simple proposition: What is a 'children's film'? Second, it draws lines of distinction between commercial and non-commercial films. And third, it outlines the historical conditions of production in countries where children's cinema is particularly well-established.

1.1 What is a 'Children's Film'?

One likely reason for the critical neglect of children's film is the purported difficulty of defining it. Ian Wojcik-Andrews believes that defining children's film is akin to untying a Gordian knot, deeming it 'something of an impossibility' (2000: 7). Another critic, M. Keith Booker, does not even think that definition is important, admitting that he is 'relatively little troubled' by the matter (2010: xv–xvi). My approach in this book is very different: I believe that it *is* possible to define children's film, and that such a definition is vital to understanding the form. This task first requires narrowing the terms of reference and sifting through different approaches to the topic. A children's film, I would suggest, is one produced and widely received as such. I will elaborate on this basic definition over the course of this chapter, but before proceeding further, it is necessary to make a distinction between films made *for children*, and films *about children*. Wojcik-Andrews, in his book *Children's Films: History, Ideology, Pedagogy, Theory*, conflates these two forms: He regards any film in which a child appears as a children's film, including explicitly adult-oriented films such as *The Exorcist* (William Friedkin, 1973), *Pixote* (Héctor Babenco, 1981) and *Kids* (Larry Clark, 1995). But although he applies the term 'children's film' to such releases, Wojcik-Andrews's monograph actually belongs to a parallel body of scholarship that explores the *representation of childhood* in popular cinema, but which is not chiefly concerned with films that are produced specifically for the consumption of children (cf. Goldstein and Zornow 1980; Merlock Jackson 1986; Sinyard 1992; Lury 2010). The more adult-oriented films he considers might more properly be called 'childhood films', a term used by scholars such as Stephanie Hemelryk Donald (2000: 48) to differentiate them from those that mostly address child audiences.

Wojcik-Andrews also suggests that films watched by children axiomatically *are* children's films. But this cannot hold water: Children consume entertainment media of all different kinds. If we take Wojcik-Andrews's principle to its fullest logical extension, any film ever made has the potential to be a children's film; as Ewan Kirkland observes, 'surely sometime, somewhere, all films have been seen by one child or another' (2004: 11). In 1993, it was reported that over 100,000 British children under the age of 15 had watched the late-night UK television premiere of the '18'-rated horror film, *Child's Play 3* (Jack Bender, 1991), a production that was not manufactured for children, not marketed towards children, not rated as suitable for children's consumption, and presumably watched only by a small minority of children (Culf 1993). In no sense is it useful to categorise it as a 'children's film', not least because its illicit attraction to these British children no doubt derived, in large part, from the perception that it is the very *opposite* of a children's film.

The impossibility of categorising films based purely on who actually watches them is further underlined by the fact that many films marketed towards children are viewed widely by adults. Indeed, most commercial films are consciously constructed to appeal equally to parents and guardians, who are usually needed to accompany younger children to the cinema. For this reason, a large percentage of 'children's films' are more properly termed 'family films'; as we shall see, these two categories overlap considerably (Brown 2012; Brown and Babington 2015). Notable producers of child-oriented films in Hollywood, including Walt Disney, Robert Radnitz and Brian Henson, have explicitly stated that they made films for audiences of *all* ages, not just children (Merlock Jackson 2006: 13–14; Scheur 1963; Weinraub 1997). This is borne out by statistics released by the Motion Picture Association of America (MPAA). In 2012, children aged 2–11 made up 12 per cent of 'frequent movie-goers' in North America; this figure fell to 7 per cent in 2013 (MPAA 2014: 12). However, 41 of the 50 highest-grossing films at the North American box office in 2012 and 2013 were deemed suitable for children (this includes films in the 'G', 'PG', and 'PG-13' categories), with only nine films rated 'R' (adult-only) (MPAA 2014: 22–23). This is a major disparity when one considers that almost 60 per cent of all theatrical releases in the United States are classified as 'R' ('Entertainment Industry': 13).

The majority of live-action Hollywood blockbusters are rated 'PG-13'. This allows children to view them with parental supervision, but it also extends appeal to the vital adolescent and teenage markets. Many 'PG-13' films, such as *The Simpsons Movie* (David Silverman, 2007) and the last five instalments in the *Harry Potter* series (2001–11), are marketed towards children under the age of 12. As Peter Krämer observes, 'most of Hollywood's superhits since 1977 are basically, like *Star Wars*, children's films; more precisely, they are children's films for the whole family and for teenagers, too' (2004: 366–67). As of late 2016, a list of the top 30 highest-grossing films ever includes such putatively child-oriented releases as *Jurassic World* (Colin Trevorrow, 2015) with $1.6 billion; *Frozen* (Chris Buck and Jennifer Lee, 2013) with $1.2 billion; *Minions* (Pierre Coffin and Kyle Balda, 2015) with $1.1 billion; *Toy Story 3* (Lee Unkrich, 2010), *Jurassic Park* (Steven Spielberg, 1993), *Alice in Wonderland* (Tim Burton, 2009), *Zootopia* (Byron Howard and Rich Moore, 2016), and *Finding Dory* (Andrew Stanton and Angus MacLane, 2016) with approximately $1 billion each; and *Despicable Me 2* (Pierre Coffin and Chris Renaud, 2013) and *The Lion King* (Roger Allers and Rob Minkoff, 1994) with just under $1 billion. Given the relatively lowly proportion of children under the age of 12 in the US theatrical audience, non-child audiences clearly play a major role in sustaining Hollywood's industry of 'children's films'.

For these reasons, the category of 'children's film' cannot be conceptualised purely in terms of what children (or adults) actually consume. In pursuing an alternative definition, as Wojcik-Andrews cautions against, we find ourselves entering murky waters; but a more precise formulation is necessary if we hope to understand the form. Otherwise – if we accept his claim to the 'impossibility' of definition – all we are left with is the dogmatically uncritical view that while *something* called a 'children's film' clearly exists, it is fundamentally unknowable. At this juncture, it is useful to turn to children's literary studies. Scholars such as Matthew Grenby argue that children's literature is 'defined by its intended audience' (2009: xiii). This idea has found sympathy in some accounts of children's cinema. Michael Newton ventures that a children's film 'is a film defined by its imagined audience' (2006: 17). Stephanie Hemelryk Donald and Kirsten Seale argue that 'a children's film is a film produced for a primary audience of children' (2013: 98). And Krämer suggests that 'children's films are films made specifically for children', particularly those 'aged twelve or younger' (2002: 186).

This view of children's film as defined by target audience is a useful and pragmatic starting point. However, it does require some elaboration.

Basing a definition solely on 'imagined audience' invests too much authority in producers and marketers, and too little in the movie-going public, which ultimately decides for itself whether a film falls into a particular category or not. But although most people seem to recognise a film 'for children' when they see one, it is not immediately obvious *how* this happens. In response to this, I would argue in favour of a *negotiated identity*. Genre, to repurpose Rick Altman's memorable phrase, does not 'spring full-blown from the head of Zeus' (2003: 29). Rather, it is constructed through a complex interaction of *textual* and *contextual* mechanisms. While genres are usually conceived of in terms of shared formal characteristics between groups of films, generic identity is also shaped by external factors. As Steve Neale observes, these include the 'discourses of publicity, promotion and reception that surround mainstream films and shape popular responses, including industry categories as well as trade and press reviews' (2000: 2–3). In a series of recent publications, scholars such as myself and Peter Krämer have applied Neale's principle to the study of children's films and family films (Brown 2012: 6–9; Brown 2013a; Krämer 2015). There are at least five contextual processes through which their generic identity is established:

1) *Marketing and distribution strategies*
Most films for children are actively marketed as such, both explicitly and implicitly, through promotional materials such as trailers, movie posters, print advertisements and press books. Unsurprisingly, marketing strategies for commercial films tend to position them to as wide an audience as possible. The press book for *The Wizard of Oz* (Victor Fleming, 1939), which was distributed to theatre managers throughout the United States, claimed that it 'Successfully combin[ed] for the first time adult and juvenile appeal in a motion picture', adding that 'Producer Mervyn LeRoy increased this all-family popularity by making the picture one hundred percent musical, with catchy tunes and clever lyrics. He next added Technicolor and amazing "magic" which will intrigue audiences of all ages'. The voiceover on the theatrical trailer for *Home Alone*, a film in which a young boy is left behind when his family go on holiday to Paris, wryly announces it as 'a family comedy without the family'. And *The Railway Children* (Lionel Jeffries, 1970), perhaps the quintessential British children's film, was (ungrammatically) promoted with the movie poster tagline: 'A Film for

Adults to Take Their Children, too!'

These promotional strategies are largely confined to commercial cinema, and are less visible in relation to non-commercial traditions such as Britain's Children's Film Foundation (CFF), the Children's Film Society of India (CFSI) or East Germany's *Deutsche Film-Aktiengesellschaft* (DEFA). Nevertheless, even in these cases, materials are sometimes available that communicate a film's content and intended audience. As is common practice in children's publishing, child-oriented films are commonly advertised (in posters and flyers distributed at film festivals, and in web pages) using bright, vibrant colours and simple, large fonts. The home page of the Indian Children's Film Society website deploys a number of colourful, apparently homemade, pictures of children, animals and other familiar childhood iconographies. Together, these work to establish, though associative cues, the organisation's identity as a producer of children's fiction.

2) *Censorship and suitability ratings*

The existence of censorship reflects an enduring perception that children (vulnerable, innocent) require protection from early exposure to disturbing content, such as physical and psychological violence, overt sexuality, frighteningly pessimistic views of life and the world, and otherwise 'adult' themes and issues. Censorship in some form – whether imposed by external systems of regulation or voluntarily adopted by producers – has been a constant in the history of film. The British Board of Film Censorship (now 'Classification') (BBFC) introduced a rudimentary version of its present-day ratings system in 1913, with films classified simply as 'U' (universal; suitable for all) or 'A' (adult; not suitable for children). Between 1934 and 1966, the Hollywood film industry was regulated by the Production Code, a self-censorship system geared to preventing 'adult' content reaching 'family' audiences. Since 1968, Hollywood has operated a more diversified ratings system, which currently comprises 'G' (suitable for all ages); 'PG' (parental guidance; some material regarded as unsuitable for children); 'PG-13' (parents strongly cautioned; some material regarded as inappropriate for children under the age of 13); 'R' (restricted; children under the age of 17 require accompanying parent/guardian); and 'NC-17' (no children under the age of 17 admitted). The merits of ratings systems have been widely debated. Many films passed for universal exhibition avoid censorious content but still articulate complex issues, focus entirely on adult characters and their preoccupations, or contain sophisticated dialogue. Equally, films deemed unsuitable for children because of 'mature' content, such as Universal's horror films of the 1930s or the *James Bond* series (1962–), sometimes appeal strongly to them.

Most countries continue to have such mechanisms in place, but their application is contingent on local customs and beliefs. For instance, the Australian family film *Babe* (Chris Noonan, 1995), which centres on an anthropomorphised pig, was initially banned in Malaysia, a country in which pigs (in keeping with Islamic doctrine) are widely considered unclean. Equally, children's films uncensored in their home nations have often been censored or banned altogether in other countries, as with Hollywood films in Soviet Russia and pre-1990s PRC China. (This works both ways: North America screens an extremely low percentage of foreign-language films.) Even in the relatively undifferentiated Western world, some systems of censorship are more stringent, and others more liberal. In France, the adult-oriented *Taxi Driver* (Martin Scorsese, 1976) was first certificated as '16', then '12'; *Eyes Wide Shut* (Stanley Kubrick, 1999) was certificated as '10'; and *Borat* (Larry Charles, 2006) as 'U'. In contrast, *Borat* was classified as 'R' in the USA, thus permitting the admittance of under-17s only when accompanied by an adult. The Scandinavian countries are also more liberal in attitudes to censorship. The Danish animated feature *Terkel in Trouble* (*Terkel i knibe*, Stefan Fjeldmark et al., 2004) – which won the Best Children's/Family award at the 2005 Copenhagen Robert Festival – has a '7' rating in Denmark and an '11' in Sweden and Norway. However, it is more conservatively rated '15' in the UK and Ireland, and 'R' in the US. Recent liberalisation reflects a growing belief, particularly in late-industrial society, that attempting to impose such restrictions on children is futile, given their ability to access knowledge, sights and sounds forbidden to previous generations through other means (cf. Simonton et al. 2013). In commercial cinema, it also bespeaks a commercially-motivated desire to appeal to the widest possible audience cross-section.

Most films exhibited at children's film festivals never receive theatrical release, and therefore do not receive an official suitability rating. Festivals often show films for children and young people up to the age of 16 or 18, and apply their own suitability ratings. The programme for the 2013 Chicago International Children's Film Festival divided its films into precisely-defined demographics: 2+, 4+, 5+, 8+, 9+, 11+ and 15+. The comparatively hermetic world of the children's film festival is the only place where film production and exhibition in the children's film field imitates television in playing to relatively narrow demographics within the overarching 'child audience'.

3) *Critical reception*

As well as offering interpretive judgements on a film's quality, reviews communicate important information such as plot, tone and character. There is historical evidence that children both in the United States and Britain have used printed reviews in determining what films they wanted to see (Miller Mitchell 1929: 58; Kesterton 1948: 54). Publications such as the 'Family Movie Guide' section in *Parents' Magazine* and the British *Monthly Film Bulletin* (*MFB*) targeted adult readers (including theatre managers), and explicitly categorised films by presumed and intended audience. The *MFB*, for instance, employed four labels: 'A' (adults only), 'B' (adults and adolescents), 'C' (family audiences) and 'D' (particularly suitable for children's performances). Today, sites such as *Movieguide*, owned by the evangelical Christian Ted Baehr, categorise and adjudge films according to their 'suitability' for children and adherence to conservative Christian doctrine. A less polemical role is performed by a global nexus of online discourses, including aggregated review sites like Metacritic and Rotten Tomatoes, blogs and forums, social media such as Twitter and Tumblr, and popular film sites such as IMDb, which categorises all films by genre.

4) *Merchandising*

In commercial cinema, a film's generic identity (or identities) can often be gauged by the merchandise associated with it. Merchandising has con-stituted a useful ancillary revenue stream since the 1930s, when Disney pioneered a hugely profitable licensing deal with Kay Kamen. Today, the majority of Western children's films above a certain budgetary level are accompanied by extensive merchandising campaigns, encompassing toys, clothes, games, music soundtracks and tie-ins with fast food or drinks manufacturers. Whilst adult films have, until recently, offered compara-tively few opportunities for merchandise, children's films and family films are particularly attractive because of their broad audience base, the par-ticular demand amongst children for toys, games, branded clothing, fast food and so on, and the additional scope for licensable properties accorded by fantastical narratives, of which child-oriented films constitute a large percentage. Commercial licensing deals (and a multimedia presence more broadly) have often been regarded as a barometer of a film's ability to transcend a narrow 'child audience' and instead reach a wider, more lucrative consumer base. Conversely, one of the most profitable 'ancillary' revenue streams in post-1990s Hollywood family franchises has been the so-called 'kidvid': films released solely on home video, often spun off from profitable theatrical releases, and specifically targeting younger children. *The Return of Jafar* (Tad Stones, 1994), Disney's direct-to-video sequel to *Aladdin* (Ron Clements and John Musker, 1994), cost only $6 million to produce, but sold seven million copies (Brown 2012: 207–8).

5) *Exhibition strategies*
Generic identity is partially determined by conditions of exhibition; specifically, *where* a film is shown and to *whom*. These include theatrical release (e.g. whether for general audiences or to children's matinees), television broadcasts (i.e. when a film is scheduled), and presence in children's film festivals worldwide.

Since the beginnings of the twentieth century, exhibitors and theatre managers have programmed special film shows for children. One early instance was a tour by the Great American Bioscope, which presented a film show in Mickleover, Great Britain, in February 1900. The screening was promoted as 'free from vulgarity throughout' and the admission fee for children was 1d., as opposed to 3d. for adult patrons (Staples 1997: 2–3). The practice of charging children reduced admission (typically half-price) was later adopted by commercial exhibitors in many countries, particularly in continental Europe and the United States. Specialised children's cinema programmes showed a wide variety of films – including shorts and features, live-action and animation, fiction and documentary – thought to be especially suited for children. However, many films viewed by children in matinees were never specifically *intended* for children's consumption. Chaplin, Harold Lloyd, Laurel and Hardy, the Three Stooges and cheap westerns starring the likes of Tom Mix, formed the basis for children's matinee programming in Britain and North America during the 1920s and 1930s (Staples 1997: 22). While a non-commercial tradition of children's cinema has never fully developed in the United States, children attending matinees and other special performances in countries such as Britain, Russia, Czechoslovakia, East Germany, China and India have, at some point, had access to films specifically produced and screened for their consumption.

Today, special theatrical programmes for children are less common. Children's film in its most child-oriented (i.e. non-commercial) form is now primarily sustained by children's film festivals. Through exhibition, and attendant publicity and prizes, festivals promote the manufacture and viewing of specialised films for children. In the majority of cases – exceptions being predominantly in the young adult category – these do not gain commercial release, but may receive further distribution through schools, clubs and, in some fortunate cases, children's slots on television. High-profile festivals include the Chicago International Children's Film Festival (1983–), the Los Angeles-based International Family Film Festival (1993–), the Seoul International Youth Film Festival (1999–) and the International Children's Film Festival, India. Between January and March 2013, others took place in Bangladesh, Hof, Seattle, Glasgow, Berlin, Antwerp and Bruges, Annonay, Val-de-Marne, Providence, Middlesbrough, Calgary, New York, Montreal, Winnipeg, Lyon, Malmö, Wurzburg, Augsburg and Bologna.

Television plays a key role in how films are represented to the public in the months and years *after* theatrical release. In Western nations, in particular, daytime television slots are reserved for programmes that possess broad audience suitability, and those shown later at night are liable to contain 'adult' elements.

Generic identity, then, is not just a matter of what appears on screen. It is subject to broader, largely uncoordinated processes of negotiation between

- producers, distributors and marketers (who sell a film);
- review boards (who adjudge its suitability for audiences and affix a 'child' or 'adult' rating);
- critics and audiences (who impose their own labels which may, or may not, accord with those supplied by film producers and distributors);
- merchandisers (licensed by studios to manufacturers of toys, games and clothing, as well as restaurant chains, all of whom sell products related to the film);
- and exhibitors (including cinema chains, television networks and film festival programmers).

Collectively, these processes play a major part in establishing and sustaining generic identity. Audiences might recognise *Frozen* as a film for children solely through contextual discourses such as movie posters, billboards and trailers, its 'PG' rating, film reviews and child-friendly (matinee or early evening) scheduling in cinemas and on television. This is not to argue that generic identity is fixed or immutable. As Krämer (2015) shows, Kubrick's *2001: A Space Odyssey* (1968) was marketed and widely received as 'film specially suitable for children' upon initial release. This initial perception of the film's child-friendliness eventually gave way to the now-familiar view of it as a quintessential 'youth film', primarily oriented to adult sensibilities. Genre labels, then, remain fluid and open-ended. They are subject to shifting historical socio-cultural norms.

Equally, contextual discourses are shaped by recognition of the *textual* elements that place films within an interpretive framework. In other words, in order for a film to be established popularly as a children's film, it must – somehow – be recognisable as such, meeting established expectations regarding what a children's film *is*. These expectations are subject to degrees of renegotiation. It is probable that the historical shift in the generic identity of *2001: A Space Odyssey* from 'family film' to 'youth film' reflects the fact that, as a piece of entertainment, it does not appear to be especially child-friendly. As such, the initial generic identity created by the film's distributor proved to be unstable. Similarly, as Jennifer Geer (2007) shows, when Miramax (then a subsidiary of Disney) released its J. M. Barrie biopic, *Finding Neverland* (Marc Foster, 2004), on DVD, the studio attempted to reposition it as a 'family film', despite the fact that it was neither promoted nor widely received as such upon theatrical release. Again, this commercially-motivated attempt to reconstitute *Finding Neverland* as a family film was largely unsuccessful. Children's cinema, then, *must* possess a set of textual and associative significations that differentiates it from cinema intended primarily for adult audiences. In very simple terms, this is why most people – not just children – know children's films when they see them.

This leads us to consider the presence of recurrent narrative, thematic and ideological features. As Bruce Babington (via Arthur Schopenhauer) has argued, critics who try to establish a set of shared characteristics in relation to any large body of texts must walk a tightrope between the laws of 'homogeneity' and 'specification' (2005: 122–23). According to these laws, we must seek unity in things without overlooking important differences.

In relation to film, homogeneity – at its most extreme – occurs when the genre's characteristics are seen as so broad, so all-encompassing, that they could apply to almost *any* film. Bettina Kümmerling-Meibauer suggests that:

> The study of children's films is a complex and demanding issue, involving a range of critical, educational, psychological, cultural, institutional, and textual aspects. 'Children's films' can be a broad and ambiguous term; there are films aimed at children, films about childhood, and films children watch regardless of whether they are children's films or films targeted toward adults. (2013: 39)

The intention behind such a broad approach, one assumes, is to widen the terms of the debate, and to acknowledge ambiguities within the category. This is a laudable goal in itself. As Kümmerling-Meibauer rightly observes, the study of children's films has often trespassed well beyond the normative boundaries of film studies – with its primary foci on film text and context – reaching into areas such as sociology (especially childhood studies), psychology, and education; these interdisciplinary methodological approaches to children and film are extremely valuable. However, the all-inclusive definitions proposed by Wojcik-Andrews and Kümmerling-Meibauer overextend the parameters of children's cinema to such a degree that connections between films become tenuous. Aside from the fact that both feature children as main characters, there is little that relates the adult-oriented horror film, *The Exorcist*, to the family-oriented musical, *Annie* (John Huston, 1982). There are grey areas in between, of course; are *The 400 Blows* (*Les Quatre Cents Coups*, François Truffaut, 1959) or *Kes* (Ken Loach, 1969) – which are grittier and more downbeat than *Annie* but lack the strongly 'adult' elements of *The Exorcist* – children's films, or simply films *about* children? Such ambiguities are why a contextual approach to genre is necessary. Placing proper emphasis on how films are promoted and received, it allows us to identify a corpus of texts widely understood as 'children's films', and to draw thematic, narrative and stylistic connections between them. In turn, this can yield important insights regarding social, cultural and ideological meanings.

The risk then becomes one of extreme specification, in which the characteristics of the genre are so tightly defined that they apply only to a very small number of films. The very mention of children's film, for instance, might evoke certain 'prototypical' story elements: the presence of children, animals, magic, and adventure; the child's learning of responsibility and coming of age. However, these elements are far from universal. Films for children inhabit a multitude of generic styles, and their cultural and ideological meanings are similarly broad-ranging. In short, children's films are inherently pluralistic. Mindful of this, I would propose five very broad but recurrent features of the children's film. These characteristics will be elaborated, and interrogated, over the course of this book:

i) The reaffirmation of family, kinship and community. Films for children, as the case studies in this book will demonstrate, routinely forge or reaffirm ties of kinship between individuals and groups of people. The most important social connections in children's films are within the family unit, particularly between children and parents. Close friendship, community and cohesion at several levels of society are also prominent, and are often manifested in a sense of pulling together in a common cause. This is true of commercial films produced in Hollywood, but is particularly evident in state-regulated systems of children's cinema, including the British CFF and the East German DEFA. In these cases, school and family are socialising apparatuses and microcosms of society-at-large; they serve to recapitulate the dominant ideology.

ii) The foregrounding of child, adolescent and teenage figures and their experiences. Most protagonists of children's films are actual children or adolescents, as embodied by young performers such as Jackie Coogan, Shirley Temple, Judy Garland, Mickey Rooney, Sabu, Macaulay Culkin and Lindsay Lohan. But the on-screen presence of children is not a pre-requisite for classification as a children's film. Instead, many productions centre on what might be called 'symbolic children': non-child figures in which 'childlike' attributes – such as innocence, goodness, unaffectedness, vulnerability and a predilection for unfettered play and misadventure – are invested. The category of symbolic child is highly mutable. It includes 'childlike' grown-ups, such as Laurel and Hardy, the Three Stooges, Pee-wee Herman, the adult protagonists of Satyajit Ray's *Goopy and Bagha* trilogy (1968–90) and the Brazilian comedy troupe, the Trapalhões; lovable animals, such as Rin Tin Tin, Lassie, Dumbo and Flipper; aliens, such as E.T.; and animated toys, like the protagonists of *Pinocchio* (Norman Ferguson et al., 1940) and

Toy Story (John Lasseter, 1995). In children's cinema, childhood is not just a biologically-determined development stage; it is a social construct.

iii) The exclusion and/or eventual defeat of disruptive social elements. Just as the protagonists of children's films are nearly always sympathetic and/or morally upstanding, it is a firm structural principle of the genre that individuals and/or groups that violate accepted codes of society will eventually get their comeuppance. In comedic films this may simply take the form of mild social embarrassment, such as the comic tropes of pies in the face, trousers falling down, or slipping on an oil slick. In more serious cases, it might involve the incarceration or death of the malefactor(s). Such punishments fulfil several ideological functions. Firstly, they provide audiences with basic reassurance (a form of cosmic balancing). Secondly, they demonstrate the efficacy of the social machinery of justice and order, specifically the rule of law, and the benevolence of the state. Thirdly, they reinforce a basic tenet of the socialisation process: that criminality or anti-social behaviour is aberrant, unprofitable and is always punishable by machineries of justice that serve collective morality.

iv) The minimisation of 'adult' representational elements. Perhaps the clearest distinguishing feature of children's cinema is the avoidance of themes or representational elements with the potential to upset, disturb or corrupt young minds. In films for children, aspects such as sex, nudity, violence, criminality, sustained pessimism, extreme profanity, drug abuse, human or animal suffering, and gore are permissible only in very limited quantities. In some traditions, certain levels of sexual innuendo or mild profanity are seen to be acceptable, particularly in the contemporary children's cinemas of more liberal nations such as the United States, Britain, France, Germany, Sweden or Denmark. But 'adult' content is always regulated. While many children's films explore complex themes, they tend to be dealt with either abstractly (e.g. through metonymy, allegory or ellipsis) or via suggestion. Violence is usually sanitised (such as bloodless gunfights) or free from consequence (e.g. slapstick fight scenes where no party is seriously injured). More traumatic realities – such as direct representations of sustained and visceral violence, terrorism, genocide, ethnic cleansing, sexual assault or paedophilia – are almost always avoided.

v) Finally, while stories may acknowledge the possibility of an unpleasant or undesirable outcome, endings are predominantly upbeat, emotionally uplifting, morally unambiguous and supportive of the social status quo. A famous example is *The Wizard of Oz*. In the final scene, Dorothy Gale (Judy Garland) returns from a magical adventure in the Land of Oz to her quiet, rural life in Kansas, surrounded by her friends and family, and newly convinced that 'There's no place like home'. The film deals with clear moral binaries, positing a straightforward battle between Dorothy and her friends (good) and the Wicked Witch (Margaret Hamilton) and her followers (evil). The eventual death of the Wicked Witch represents the restoration of order and benign rule. Dorothy's longed-for return to Kansas provides narrative closure; it sees her restored to a comfortable and loving domestic setting, eliminating the potentially disquieting possibility that the Oz interlude was a real-life adventure and rationalising it merely as a child's fantasy. Furthermore, here, as in most children's films and family films, the emotional uplift associated with what is crudely (but rarely inaccurately) termed the 'happy ending' is interspersed with – and heightened by – relief that a seemingly inevitable tragic or unpleasant ending has been averted.

To these overarching conventions, further specifications can be added in relation to sub-genres such as children's fairy tale films, adventure films, animal films, and numerous other forms. But it is important to note that recurring features in the children's film do not reflect (at least not solely) children's preferred patterns of fantasy, or even to what producers believe children wish to see in their screen entertainment. They are prescribed by what (adult) society believes children *ought to see* – a determination that is based on social, psychological, ethical and behavioural considerations. Children's film is an invention of adult society. As such, it is hardly surprising that these conventions are most apparent in films intended for younger children, but progressively less visible in films intended for older children (particularly those above the age of about 12). In the 'teen film' – a genre that might be thought of as a close relative of the 'children's film' but actually, in some regards, is *antithetical* to it – they may be entirely absent. Films intended for adolescents are a greyer area. Some 'youth' films, such as those produced in Denmark for young people up to the age of 18, are closer in style and representation to 'adult' dramas than to children's films. For this reason, these 'teen' or 'youth' films fall outside the scope of this book.

But even in films intended primarily for younger children (as opposed to adolescents or teenagers), the textual characteristics listed above are neither inviolable nor immutable. Most readers will be able to bring to mind films that violate at least one of these conventions. For instance, the extraordinary Hollywood production, *5,000 Fingers of Dr. T* (Roy Rowland, 1953), subverts expectations that narrative cinema – and, more particularly, children's film – should be 'transparent' in its storytelling; it is wilfully hard to follow, and is suffused with logical discontinuities, obscure symbolism and nonsense dialogue. Equally, a 'happy ending' is widely perceived as a necessary component of children's cinema, but films like *My Girl* (Howard Zieff, 1991) and *Tarka the Otter* (David Cobham, 1979) deliberately confound this expectation by ending with the tragic death of their protagonists. Similarly, towards the end of films such as *The Snowman* (Dianne Jackson, 1982) and *Old Yeller* (Robert Stevenson, 1957), the child protagonist must come to terms with the death of a beloved companion. (Successfully coping with such tragedies, however, relates to another recurrent trope of children's cinema: that of the child's psychological coming-of-age.) And *Terkel in Trouble*, which was given a child-friendly rating in its native Denmark, is replete with gross-out humour and profanity, to the extent that in countries with less liberal censorship (including Britain and the United States) it is generally regarded as an 'adult' animation. Incongruities such as these tend to attract comment or surprise precisely *because* they are aberrant within the larger conventions of the genre.

Of course, changes in convention reflect the wider mutability of children's culture and childhood, as well as considerations of commerce and morality. In European non-commercial children's cinema of the 1940s and 1950s, it was widely accepted that films should employ relatively simple film syntax, avoiding techniques of 'distantiation' such as discontinuous narrative, montage editing, flashbacks and jump cuts. Henri Storck's UNESCO report on children's entertainment films, published in 1950, drew attention to 'the crucial problem' of 'artistic direction' (73–74), and Mary Field of the British Children's Film Foundation argued that 'the editing of a children's film requires [...] controlled simplicity and clarity' (1952: 95). These views are no longer as predominant. Numerous post-1970s Hollywood family films also push boundaries of acceptability for children's consumption, with stronger portrayals of violence and greater degrees of moral ambiguity (the *Harry Potter* films are an obvious example).

Another trend in post-1970s Hollywood films is the predominance of teenage or young adult protagonists. Although children are at the centre of many recent family films, such as *Frozen* and *Harry Potter*, live-action franchises with teen and adult appeal, including the *Star Wars* (1977–), *The Lord of the Rings* (2001–2003) and the Marvel Cinematic Universe series (2008–), tend to centre on young people on the cusp of adulthood. These are characters to whom adolescent and teenage audiences can identify, and to whom younger children can aspire. The Hollywood teen exploitation studio, AIP, recognised this fact as long ago as the 1950s when it developed a syllogism called 'The Peter Pan Syndrome', which held that 'a younger child will watch anything an older child will watch', but that 'an older child will not watch anything a younger child will watch' (Doherty 2002: 128).

Relatedly, Hollywood 'tween' films such as Disney's *High School Musical* series (2006–08) have generic affiliations both to the children's film (the avoidance of strongly 'adult' representational elements; the narrative focalisation on children; the happy ending) and to the teen film (the emphasis on sexual awakenings and emotional maturation). The emergence of the 'tween film' responds to changing definitions of childhood in Western societies, in which the *non-biological* onset of 'adulthood' is seen to occur at an earlier age than in previous generations. In both the 'tween film' and the 'family film', younger children remain vital to commercial profitability. However, both forms employ a range of textual strategies to broaden the appeal base beyond that of pre-adolescent children, including the addition of jokes, allusions, themes, sub-plots, adult stars and more sophisticated humour (e.g. wordplay or innuendo). It is also worth noting that commercial family films are far less likely to be explicitly moralistic or educational than non-commercial and/or state-funded children's films.

In generic terms, children's films and family films are best regarded as partially distinct, but predominantly overlapping, 'master-genres'. The concept of the master-genre is akin to the Platonic and Aristotelian 'modes' which, in literary criticism, have provided 'fixed points' against which 'genres' – which are more thematic, and are linked to changing socio-historical contexts – are understood. Thus, the ahistorical, non-thematic categories of 'the comic', 'the tragic', 'the heroic', 'the satirical', 'the romantic', 'the melodramatic' and 'the gothic' are all modes, whereas the greater specificity and temporality of 'film noir' (prototypically 1940s) or 'the slasher film' (post-1970s) delineates them as genres.

In the 'children's film', a broad, formally diverse array of sub-genres may operate; but if a film addresses child audiences, it must satisfy certain structural expectations popularly associated with entertainment for children. Child-oriented films also frequently cross over from live-action cinema to animation, a form that includes traditional cel animation, puppet animation, stop-motion animation and computer-generated animation. Just as modes such as 'comedy' or 'tragedy' may be channelled into a wide array of generic forms, children's cinema is generically diverse. The following Hollywood child-oriented films all possess distinct multigeneric identities: *Snow White* (fairy tale); *National Velvet* (animal film); *Mary Poppins* (musical); *E.T.* (sci-fi); *Back to the Future III* (western); *Who Framed Roger Rabbit* (*film noir*); *Mrs. Doubtfire* (comedy); and *Harry Potter* (fantasy). They may be approached from multiple standpoints; equally, each of them is locatable within (and, to a degree, bound by) the conventions of children's cinema, which functions here as the master-genre.

At this point, it is useful to think of the children's film and the family film in terms of the semantic/syntactic approach to genre proposed by Tzvetan Todorov, and advocated by Fredric Jameson, Rick Altman and others. Film's semantic aspects are those discernible on surface viewing; they include recurring character types, locations, sets, props, shots, lighting, music, mood and tone, camera set-ups, editing patterns and *mise-en-scène*. Most scholarly accounts of film genre have gravitated towards semantic commonalities. For example, *film noir* is seen to be characterised as much by lighting (chiaroscuro), character (detectives; femme fatales), setting (metropolitan criminal underworld), props (pistols; cigarettes) and mood (oppressive; downbeat) as by story type or political orientation. Syntactic aspects are harder to define. They include overall narrative patterns and story structures, as well as ritual, cultural and ideological meanings. Semantic approaches are applicable mostly to genres with instantly recognisable, and relatively fixed, iconographies, such as the western. They may also be applied to individual *sub-genres* and *cycles* within the broader categories of children's films and family films. However, semantic aspects are heavily related to historically-bound questions of cinematic style and socio-cultural convention. Children's films and family films are international in their provenance, and because stylistic conventions are both highly changeable and inextricably linked with local cultural tradition, there is considerable semantic variation across their wider histories.

A genre's syntactic aspects are usually less changeable. Indeed, the narrative principles, ideological resonances, and cultural meanings of children's films have remained relatively stable. Despite ongoing changes in culture and society, most continue to adhere to established conventions: they reaffirm family, friendship and community; they foreground real or symbolic children; they marginalise disruptive social elements, or engage with them in order to defeat them; they downplay 'adult' themes and situations; their narratives are relatively straightforward, easily grasped and negate ambiguity; and, ultimately, they work to uphold social norms, create emotional uplift and engender kinship. As with all modes of fiction, ongoing changes in culture and society impose modifications to some of these conventions without violating them altogether. Consensus regarding what is deemed acceptable for children's consumption has continued to shift, in conjunction with ongoing liberalising currents in Western society. Britain's Children's Film Foundation (1951–85), initially a paragon of middlebrow values, grew progressively bolder in addressing potentially hard-hitting subjects (such as domestic violence) during the 1970s and 1980s. Equally, the last five entries in the *Harry Potter* series received 'PG-13' ratings in the United States, reflecting their stronger representations of violence, moral ambiguity, mild sexual content and occasional profanity. But the point is that, in spite of changes in culture and society, children's films continue to be measured against a widely-accepted generic framework – linked to social constructions of childhood – that delineates what they are, and what they are not.

1.2 Pedagogy and Pleasure

As Bazalgette and Staples argue, the prevailing antithesis in child-oriented cinema is between commercial and non-commercial productions (1995: 94–95). Commercial films are governed by the pleasure principle, and are predicated on the economic necessity of attracting as broad an audience as possible. As such, their producers generally utilise textual strategies aimed to transcend their base audience of children. This is because the 'child audience' – defined by Bazalgette and Staples (ibid.), Brown and Babington (2015: 2) and Rössler et al. (2009: 2) as largely encompassing children under the age of 12 – is usually considered too small to guarantee profitability. Furthermore, the variously-defined 'tween', 'teen' and 'youth' films have generally been construed as distinct from children's films, addressing more financially-independent adolescent/teen audiences wishing to graduate from what Krämer has called 'the children's ghetto' (2002: 193). This desire is reflected in the well-documented practice of older children sneaking into age-restricted movies, and, indeed, in the popularity of such Hollywood 'tween' (i.e. pre-teen or early-teen) films as the *High School Musical*, *Twilight* (2008–12) and *Hunger Games* (2012–16) series. The relative inaccessibility of the enormously lucrative teen market, the perceived unprofitability of the narrowly-conceived 'child audience', and the desire to appeal to parents accompanying children to the cinema all necessitate, in mainstream popular cinema, a multi-layered mode of address calculated to secure a broad, trans-demographic clientele.

Non-commercial children's films have typically been made under pedagogical principles, aimed at inculcating certain moral and behavioural practices. There is a long history of films aimed at children made for explicitly didactic purposes within systems of state-regulated propaganda. These include the fairy tale and animated films produced by the internationally renowned Soviet studios, *Soiuzmul'tfilm* and *Soiuzdetfilm*; animation produced in various quarters between 1933 and 1945 under the German Third Reich; the children's films produced by the state-run, socialist production company DEFA in the German Democratic Republic (GDR, or East Germany); post-war Czech puppet films, as produced by the likes of Jiří Trnka (the so-called 'Walt Disney of Eastern Europe') under the auspices of the Czechoslovak Film Institute (Československý filmový ústav, ČSFÚ); and the more formally diverse productions of the Beijing-based China Children's Film Studio (CCFS), founded by the Chinese Ministry of Culture in 1981. Post-war Czech and Russian animation, in particular, received international critical recognition for their aesthetic qualities, and were screened in Western European children's film festivals and matinee shows. In such cases, these primarily non-commercial films returned modest profits to the socialist coffers (Skupa 2015: 205–06).

Non-commercial children's films have also been produced for largely non-political purposes. Britain's Children's Film Foundation and the Children's Film Society, India (1955–) were borne through a paternalistic governmental conviction that children should be offered films that meet their specific psychological and ethical needs, as well as their aesthetic sensibilities. While the creation and development of the Russian *Soiuzmul'tfilm*, the British CFF and the Indian CFSI reflected a more interventionist phase of socialist government anathema to free market economics and laissez-faire social policy, state support of specialised children's films on a more modest, partly commercial footing remains commonplace in continental Europe, particularly in Scandinavia. In such cases, children's films are perceived locally as important expressions of cultural identity, and as necessary antidotes to the international commercialisation of children's culture. However, as with the overwhelming majority of children's films, commercial or otherwise, their ritual function has been to engender comradeship and broadly uphold principles of state and civil society.

The different modes of audience address in non-commercial and commercial children's films are worth elaborating. Essentially, there are three basic forms of address in child-oriented films: i) *single address*, where the target audience is restricted to children; ii) *double* or *dual address*, which attempts to engage both child and adult audiences, but as *separate entities*, requiring their own specific forms of engagement; and iii) *undifferentiated address*, where child and adult audiences are addressed as a *single entity* (Brown and Babington 2015: 8–10). These forms, it should be noted, are adapted from the children's literary scholar Barbara Wall's (1991) categories, which were conceived in relation to literary texts. 'Single address' is almost entirely restricted to non-commercial children's films, where there is little or no economic imperative to engage with a multidemographic audience. 'Dual address' rests on the widespread conviction among commercial producers that children and adults require different forms of entertainment based on their respective interpretative skills, knowledge and experience. Finally, 'undifferentiated address' has become more prevalent since the 1970s, reflecting a wider blurring in Western societies of the cultural distinctions between childhood and adulthood.

If 'single address' is the near-exclusive province of children's films aimed at very young audiences, Bazalgette and Staples suggest that the primary difference between this form and the more commercial 'family film' lies with casting. That is, children's films are seen as centring on a child protagonist (and thus starring a child actor), and as offering 'mainly or entirely a child's point of view' (1995: 96). In films purely intended for children, then, the child functions as narrative focaliser; events are experienced, almost entirely, from their perspective, which is shared by the spectator. In contrast, family films – particularly those produced in Hollywood – typically employ major adult stars for the benefit of mature audiences, and these adult performers take emphasis away from the child. In these cases, either there is no single point of identification, or else identification is primarily invested in adults, rather than children. Examples include the preoccupation with the aged Peter Pan as played by Robin Williams in *Hook* (Steven Spielberg, 1991), and the shared focus on each member of the family in productions such as *Meet Me in St. Louis* (Vincente Minnelli, 1944) and *The Sound of Music* (Robert Wise, 1965). At the opposite extreme, films such as Albert Lamorisse's celebrated French production, *The Red Balloon* (*Le Ballon Rouge*, 1956), centre exclusively on the experiences of the child protagonist. By the same token, while adult characters do recur as figures of guidance and protection in the productions of the CFF and CFSI, all of their films revolve around the experiences of individual or groups of children.

'Single address' is a problematic category. Regardless of whether (adult) producers *intend* their films to be viewed only by children – and childhood itself is hardly homogenous – adults may find aspects that appeal to them. Scholars of the Hollywood (Booker 2010; Brown 2012), British (Brown 2016), Russian (Pontieri 2013) and East German (Blessing 2014) cinemas have all strongly emphasised the multilayeredness of films supposedly intended primarily, or exclusively, for younger children. Mark Twain intuited this fact in his preface to *The Adventures of Tom Sawyer* (1876):

> Although my book is intended mainly for the entertainment of boys and girls, I hope it will not be shunned by men and women on that account, for part of my plan has been to pleasantly remind adults of what they once were themselves, and of how they felt and thought and talked and what queer enterprises they sometimes engaged in.

This may be taken as a classic exposition of children's fiction (literature, later film) operating through what appears to be single address (through the child focalisation and emphasis on childhood misadventure), but which is actually interpretable in multiple ways. Indeed, part of the appeal of children's fiction for adults is that of nostalgia for their own childhood – a nostalgia that child spectators cannot possibly experience or identify with.

Nonetheless, this is distinct from dual address, in which multilayered narratives are constructed to appeal to the sensibilities of adults as well as children. Sometimes such appeal is merely located in the provision of multiple identification figures: *Meet Me in St. Louis* offers episodic vignettes (micronarratives) centring, respectively, on each member of a multi-generational family. However, dual address may also take the form of materials that will not alienate children but which only adults can fully grasp. Sophisticated and sometimes suggestive wordplay or visual puns are common means of engaging adults. In the Ian Fleming-derived British production, *Chitty Chitty Bang Bang* (Ken Hughes, 1968), the heroine's name, 'Truly Scrumptious', can be appreciated wholly innocently, but for adults (with Fleming's Bond girls in mind), she partakes of the libidinousness of names such as Pussy Galore and Plenty O'Toole. A common strategy in dual-addressed family films is combining visual and verbal appeal. In Pixar's *Toy Story*, for instance, Mr. Potato Head's face is misaligned by the human baby, whereupon he quips to another of the toys, 'I'm Picasso'. He gets the reply, which stands for the child's response, 'I don't get it'. For viewers (especially children) who do not understand the joke, there is the visual comedy of the misaligned face. In the same film, a pair of detached, stereotypically female legs can be seen walking about; the legs have a large hook attached to them, signifying, for the adult, 'hooker'. Another strategy, now widely associated with contemporary Hollywood animation, is the brief, punctuating, typically comically-allusive 'cultural reference'. Unobtrusive examples include the robots in *Wall-E* (Andrew Stanton, 2008) making noises resembling the Macintosh computer start-up chime, and the elderly protagonist's conscious resemblance to Spencer Tracy in *Up* (Pete Docter, 2009).

Undifferentiated address reflects a contrary belief in the *overlapping* entertainment requirements of adults and children. Walt Disney claimed that his films addressed children of all ages, recuperating 'that fine, clean, unspoiled spot down deep in every one of us that maybe the world has made us forget and that maybe our pictures can help us recall' (Merlock Jackson 2006: 14). Many big-budget family films, such as the *Star Wars* series, heavily privilege visual spectacle and fast-paced, transparent narrative structures, and are consumed by audiences of all ages. Critic Robin Wood saw these as 'children's films conceived and marketed largely for adults', thus constructing 'the adult spectator as a child, or, more precisely, as a childish adult, an adult who would like to be a child' (1986: 163). Such films, and their adult consumers, have also been termed 'kidult'. The latter term suggests a temporary hybridisation of child and (infantilised) adult, a condition viewed widely with distaste. But as Krämer and Brown postulate, adults may actively choose to be 'regressed' in this fashion (Krämer 1998: 297; Brown 2012: 172).

Consumption of such texts does not automatically connote 'childishness', cultural illiteracy or imbecility, but may reflect a desire temporarily to escape the social and interpretive bounds of adulthood. For adults, the pleasure of such texts could well be in the exchange of what Freud called the 'debt to life with which we are burdened from our birth' (1995: 229) for a pre-sexual world of friendship, adventure and unaffectedness. Relatedly, many films evince a childish playfulness, channelled through whimsy, nonsense and scatology. Slapstick, comical linguistic excess (e.g. the cowardly lion's 'rhinoceros/impoceros' slippage in *The Wizard of Oz*), rudeness (e.g. Mr. Potato Head's implied 'kiss my ass' gesture to Woody when he removes his plastic lips and bumps them repeatedly against his posterior in *Toy Story*) and toilet humour (e.g. a feminised Robin Williams in *Mrs. Doubtfire* [Chris Columbus, 1993] caught standing up to urinate by his horrified son) all evoke a child's artless obliviousness to, or active enjoyment in, social-behavioural transgression. While people of any age may find enjoyment in these modes of comedy, studies of children's humour development have suggested that children over the age of eight tend to find 'more cognitively challenging' humour – i.e. that which requires 'work' to understand it – to be funnier than simpler forms, such as visual incongruity or nonsense wordplay. By the pre-adolescent (age 9–12) stage children also find greater pleasure in 'inside jokes', or 'metahumour', of the kind that predominate in contemporary Hollywood animated features (Cunningham 2005: 106–08). In many cases, then – particularly in the mainstream arena, where films are audience-tested rigorously to ensure that they appeal to the broadest cross-section – the hypothetical boundaries between 'single', 'dual', and 'undifferentiated' address prove to be unstable.

1.3 History and Geography

Children's cinema has always operated within larger contexts of children's culture and popular culture. John Stephens and Robyn McCallum state:

The principal domains in children's literature include biblical literature and related religious stories; myths; hero stories; medieval and quasi-medieval romance; stories about Robin Hood, which constitute a large and distinctive domain; folktales and fairy tales; oriental stories, usually linked with The Arabian Nights; and modern classics. (1998: 5–6)

Children's film is drawn from at least an equally diverse array of 'pre-texts' across a range of social, artistic, theatrical and filmic movements. The primary pre-texts for *adapted* children's films encompass classic children's books (e.g. *Alice in Wonderland*); contemporary children's, Young Adult (YA) and crossover fiction (e.g. *Harry Potter*, *The Hunger Games*); wholesome literary classics for mainstream audiences (e.g. the works of Charles Dickens, Mark Twain and Robert Louis Stevenson); fantasy and sci-fi literature (e.g. C. S. Lewis, Jules Verne); folk and fairy tales (e.g. the works of Charles Perrault, the Brothers Grimm and Hans Christian Andersen); comic books (e.g. *Tintin, Asterix, Superman*); stage properties (e.g. the works of Shakespeare); and multimedia brands (e.g. Minions, Angry Birds, Transformers and Pirates of the Caribbean).

Until recently, much of the writing on children's film has been concerned with the relation between cinema and its literary pre-texts. Although this has resulted in some fine scholarship, the need to move beyond adaptation as the primary point of entry to children's cinema was advocated by Carole Cox as far back as 1982. This is because such an approach has tended to presuppose that film for children is largely a 'text in performance' (that is, a live-action analogue of the written word), and this risks occluding the unique formal properties and industrial conditions of the medium. Furthermore, a high proportion of child-oriented films are not adaptations at all. Hollywood films and franchises such as *Star Wars, E.T.* (Steven Spielberg, 1982), *Indiana Jones* (1981–2008), *Back to the Future* (1985–90), and *Toy Story* are based on original screenplays (although, like all films, they are inherently *intertextual*). Such films are often then reconfigured as multimedia brands, being adapted themselves into novels and graphic novels, video games, toys and various other forms of ancillary merchandise. In other words, children's films operate within a nexus of cultural exchange that transcends the simplistic binary of 'source text' and 'adapted text'.

The earliest children's films were examples of what Tom Gunning (1990) calls the 'cinema of attraction', designed to showcase the aesthetic potentiality of the film medium. Commercial cinema began in late December 1895, when the Lumière brothers, Auguste and Louis, held their first public screening of projected motion pictures for a paying public at the Grand Café, Paris. Among the ten shorts on display was *L'Arroseur arrosé* (*The Sprinkler Sprinkled*, 1895), a 49-second film in which a young boy turns a garden hose on a grown-up gardener, and is rewarded for his impertinence with a smacked bottom. Kathy Merlock Jackson has identified this modest offering as the first 'children's film', and it dates to the very beginnings of cinema as a commercial proposition (1986: 31). French illusionist and filmmaker Georges Méliès produced possibly the first children's narrative fiction film, a six-minute adaptation of *Cinderella* (Fr. *Cendrillon*), in 1899. Méliès was an early pioneer of the fantasy film, and his wonderful shorts *A Trip to the Moon* (*Le Voyage dans la Lune*, 1902) and *The Impossible Voyage* (*Voyage à travers l'impossible*, 1904) remain cherished instances of early narrative cinema. Fantastic subjects such as these availed the possibility of elaborate 'trick' photographic effects, and were popular among a broad cross-section of audiences. Adapting child-friendly literary classics also brought respectability and prestige to the new medium. The early British film mogul, Cecil Hepworth, produced the earliest cinematic adaptation of *Alice in Wonderland* as an eight-minute short in 1903. In 1911, the Italian filmmaker Giulio Antamoro produced the first film version of *Pinocchio*, beating Walt Disney to Carlo Collodi's story by almost three decades. Legendary Hollywood pioneer D. W. Griffith produced one of the earliest North American explicitly child-oriented films, *The Adventures of Dollie*, in 1908. By the 1910s, Hollywood silent-era screen icon Mary Pickford was starring in a series of adaptations of children's literary classics, including *Cinderella* (1914), *The Poor Little Rich Girl* (1917), *Rebecca of Sunnybrook Farm* (1917), *The Little Princess* (1917), *Pollyanna* (1920) and *Little Lord Fauntleroy* (1921). Jackie Coogan starred in Chaplin's *The Kid* the same year.

There are many further examples of child-oriented films from cinema's silent era. A large proportion of them focused on child stars or animals (such as Rin Tin Tin), while others were adapted from established, family-friendly literary classics. Few, however, were tailor-made for children; most were intended for a 'mixed' clientele comprising both children and adults – the so-called 'family audience'. During this formative period, production of such films was largely confined to North America and to Western Europe, particularly France, Germany and Britain. However, in the years after the development of sound cinema in the early 1930s, there was greater recognition in many countries that children and adults required their own distinct entertainment spaces. Adult-oriented films began to predominate; censorship increased, as did the provision of separate children's cinema shows ('matinees'); and the production of purpose-made children's films became an industry in itself (Brown 2013b).

Within its own narrow field, scholarship on children's cinema has been as remiss as film studies more widely in focusing its attentions primarily on Western nations. While children's film was part of the fabric of commercial cinema from an early date in the United States, Britain, and much of continental Europe, not all national cinemas have an extensive history in the production of child-oriented films. In general, a flourishing tradition of children's cinema is dependent on several factors: a cultural belief that (indigenous) children's culture, and children's cinema specifically, is important and desirable; an industrial manufacturing and distribution base; the availability of creative talent; and a ready-made market for the consumption of such films. In commercial cinema, this market is usually a paying audience; in non-commercial cinema, generally it takes the form of organised performances for children (e.g. matinees, festival exhibitions or screenings in schools). A further requirement is a political will to permit or to facilitate such production. In state-supported systems, this typically rests on recognition of the potential ideological value of children's films, or a paternalistic desire to meet children's particular ethical, behavioural and entertainment needs. The most basic prerequisite, of course, is an industrial base for manufacture and distribution. During the early silent era, such conditions were largely restricted to countries such as North America, continental Europe and Russia. It was soon realised by commercial producers that children were among cinema's most enthusiastic patrons. In Britain and North America, where children's price of admittance tended to be lower (usually half-price), they attended in vast numbers. Precise comparative figures are unavailable, but a 1917 survey of cinema-going in London, and Alice Miller Mitchell's 1929 survey of children's cinema-going in Chicago, both found that over 90 per cent of school-aged children regularly attended movie theatres ('The Cinema' li; Miller Mitchell 19). In short, the commercial conditions necessary to exploit child audiences were clearly present in both countries. An important caveat is that, in both Britain and North America until the 1930s, children were rarely addressed as an independent demographic. Even the most child-friendly productions of the period were rarely shown in isolation, but formed part of a larger package of shorts and feature films typically between two-to-three hours in length. Exhibitors presented a 'balanced programme' of attractions to appeal to mixed audiences.

In the 1930s, after the coming of sound, the feature film became the dominant form in North America and most of Europe, and child-oriented shorts began to decline. In the US, in particular, the 'family audience' was the major driver of commercial cinema, as studios pursued types of film capable of appealing to 'everyone'. The child actors Shirley Temple and Mickey Rooney were Hollywood's top box office stars for seven consecutive years between 1935 and 1941, and Disney's first feature, *Snow White and the Seven Dwarfs* (David Hand et al., 1937), was the second highest-grossing film of the decade in North America. While Hollywood productions intended exclusively for children have mainly been confined to the cheap series and serials of the 1930s and 1940s, the family film has been central to Hollywood's operations from the very beginning. Disney has been a leading presence in Hollywood since the 1930s, and it has always been predicated on the manufacture and distribution of family entertainment. Since the 1970s, the other major Hollywood studios have pursued the 'family audience' with greater intensity.

The production of children's films in the Soviet Union and its satellites rested on recognition of the propagandist potential of popular cinema. While some children's films were made in Imperial Russia, it was under the Soviet system (1922–91) that production was expanded and institutionalised. As Alexander Prokhorev observes: 'Leaders of the Russian revolution viewed Soviet cinema as an essential tool of education and propaganda for the illiterate masses, above all, children' (2008: 129). In the process, he argues, children's films in Russia 'instantiated such key myths of Soviet children's culture as the dominance of the collective over the individual, child's sacrifice as the formative moment for a new ideological community, and the primacy of a child communist as the icon of the coming utopia in the profane present' (2008: 130). During the 1920s, Soviet children's films attempted to compete on a commercial footing with more popular Hollywood imports, such as the Douglas Fairbanks features that a 1929 audience survey showed were most popular amongst Russian children: *The Mark of Zorro* (Fred Niblo, 1920) and *The Thief of Bagdad* (Raoul Walsh, 1924). However, in the mid-1930s, Stalinist children's cinema was freed from the commercial mandate, and re-organised as an exclusively propagandist operation. Specialised children's movie theatres were built, and in 1936, *Soiuzdetfilm* (Studio of Children's Cinema) and *Soiuzmul'tfilm* (Studio of Cel Animation Films for Children) were formally established. Russian children's cinema continued on this state-subsidised basis until shortly prior to the collapse of the Soviet Union, as did children's film in East Germany and Czechoslovakia.

A very different political context underpins the production of child-oriented films in Iran, where numerous exponents of the post-1980s New Iranian Cinema have constructed internationally-acclaimed films around children. Abbas Kiarostami's *Where is the Friend's Home?* (*Khane-ye doust kodjast?*, 1987), Majid Majidi's *Children of Heaven* (*Bacheha-Ye aseman*, 1997) and Samira Makhmalbaf's *The Apple* (*Sib*, 1998) are notable examples of a larger trend in Iranian art cinema, in which child characters are used to articulate contentious political statements. Censorship in Iran is particularly heightened in relation to the treatment of politics and theocracy, and portrayals of sexuality and women. All three films are small-scale, naturalistic stories, set in rural townships or the poorer suburbs of Tehran. The casting and direction of non-professional child actors, and the slow, unsensational action and pacing differentiate them from the Western model of children's films. Nevertheless, Kiarostami was ambivalent about whether his own child-oriented films are *for*, or merely, *about*, children. He admitted that children grow impatient with the slow, unhurried pace of *Where is the Friend's Home?* but posited that the film may engender greater mutual understanding between children and parents who watch the film together (Bazalgette and Staples 1995: 103). Unlike the officially sanctioned children's films produced in the Soviet Union, Iranian child-centred art films have often served to unsettle, rather than reaffirm, the socio-political status quo.

In several cases, state-supported programmes of children's film have been instituted in response to the perceived failure of commercial cinema to fulfil its civic responsibilities in providing appropriate content for young minds. Mahatma Ghandi famously denounced cinema as a 'sinful technology', and in 1939, the future Indian Prime Minister, Jawaharlal Nehru, spoke of his dissatisfaction at the moral standard of popular Indian cinema, and of the need for 'high class films which have educational and social values' (Ganti 2004: 45–46). The initial push for a children's film movement in India came shortly after independence. In 1951, the government-appointed Film Enquiry Committee recommended state sponsorship of children's films, reflecting the perceived importance of educating the nation's children. Nehru was a firm supporter, arguing that:

> There is one thing, I feel, India has been lacking in, and that is children's films. Films which are really children's films are of high importance [...] Good children's films can be a very powerful instrument in developing the child, and I hope that the Indian film industry will think of this. (Agrawal and Aggarwal 1989: 188)

Through Nehru's intervention, in 1955 the Children's Film Society, India, was formed as a state-funded but artistically-autonomous body charged with producing, exhibiting and distributing films for children.

At the time of writing, the Society has produced over 250 feature films, shorts and documentaries in multiple languages, which are shown mainly in Indian schools and in children's film festivals worldwide. As is often the case with non-commercial children's cinema, such films lack systematic avenues of distribution, and thus are inaccessible to the majority of Indian children. While commercial Indian cinema – particularly Hindi films produced and distributed in Mumbai, and popularly known as 'Bollywood' – has considerable reach, until recently it has shown little interest in child-oriented films. Production has been inhibited by the widespread belief that such films are not only unprofitable, but also unnecessary, as India's censorship system ostensibly prevents content that might be 'harmful' to children from reaching screens.

The development of children's cinema in the United Kingdom is atypical, in that there are extensive traditions both in commercial and non-commercial production. Early British film history followed Hollywood in producing films for an overarching 'family audience', and many of the subjects were strikingly similar. As in the United States, literary adaptations, animal films and child-star films were produced in large numbers during the silent era. Similarly, the post-1930 surge in adult-oriented films (notably sex films and crime thrillers) led to a series of investigations of children's cinema-going that provoked considerable public anxiety, leading to a tightening of censorship restrictions intended to return the screen to a more acceptable, family-friendly footing. However, in the United States this drive to 'clean up' the screen coincided with a new and profitable wave of child-friendly productions (including Shirley Temple's vehicles). The absence of such a tendency in 1930s British cinema eventually moved the commercial film mogul J. Arthur Rank to establish Children's Entertainment Films (CEF), which he tasked with producing non-commercial short films for children's matinee exhibition that would 'do [children] good' (Staples 1997: 90–91). After seven years, Rank was forced to close the unprofitable CEF, but by this point, the government-appointed Wheare Committee had published its report into the matter of children's cinema-going, which attached 'the greatest importance' to the continuing production of non-commercial children's films (1950: 2, 28). The Children's Film Foundation was formally established as a non-profit-making, independent organisation in June 1951. The CFF was financed through a tax (the 'Eady Levy') on theatre admissions in Britain. As such, until the Thatcher government's abolition of the Eady Levy in 1985, the CFF was financially autonomous and relatively secure.

Children's cinema in Scandinavia is especially well established. Its perceived importance is twofold: it is regarded both as a socialising apparatus and as a revanchist tool in reasserting national identity and local custom in defiance of perceived US cultural imperialism. With its relatively small consumer market and lack of advanced international distribution avenues, Scandinavian children's cinema is heavily reliant on subsidies. A 2008 article published in the European Children's Film Association's *ECFA Journal* addressed the issue of the 'visibility' of home-grown child-oriented productions in a market dominated by Hollywood family movies. It lamented a 'lack of money and a lack of screens', with public broadcasters injecting fewer funds, and multiplexes cinema chains gravitating towards blockbusters (Hermans et al. 2008: 1–3).

In Denmark, frequently cited as the European country most committed to children's and youth film production, children's films have remained a major part of the structure and prestige of Danish cinema. Since 1982, under the Danish Film Act, at least 25 per cent of subsidies for film production are given to films (including documentaries and shorts) for children and youth aged 6–18. Though the level of support – just over €20 million for feature film production and development and around €6 million for shorts – is relatively slight, it remains essential for continued production. Because shorts do not reach cinemas, the Danish Film Institute oversees DVD distribution and online streaming to libraries, schools and other institutions, including the approximately 70 film clubs showing films to around 60,000 children and young people. Charlotte Giese, head of the Danish Film Institute's Children and Youth department, has said that 'it means a lot to us that Danish children are watching Danish films' (Vivarelli 2007).

In some nations, children's cinema has failed to develop into a consistent production avenue. This may be attributed to several factors. In the United States, films intended exclusively for children are considered commercially non-viable, particularly in light of the ongoing production of family-oriented films. In Middle-Eastern countries, the lack is partially attributable to a cultural distaste for juvenility. In France and Japan, meanwhile, other forms of children's culture more strongly prevail. Guy Austin has speculated that the *bande dessinée* – the comic book – has provided a 'national outlet' for children's fiction in France and Belgium (2008: 143–44). This may also be true of Japan, where both manga and anime are produced for and consumed by audiences of all ages and backgrounds.

Children's cinema globally has become increasingly commercialised. The state-backed children's cinemas of Britain and the Soviet Union faltered in the international climate of economic liberalism in the 1980s. While the Indian CFSI and the Danish Children and Youth department still operate, their subsidies are extremely low. Since the late 1990s, British studios such as Working Title, Heyday and Aardman have co-produced major international family films with Hollywood studios. Aardman and Heyday (which produced the *Harry Potter* film series) have also entered into partnerships with the Paris-based StudioCanal, thus competing with Hollywood on the global market. The French-German-Italian *Asterix & Obelix vs. Caesar* (*Astérix & Obélix contre César*, Claude Zidi, 1999) was, at the time of production, the most expensive European film ever. Targeting international family audiences, it was a major international hit (Brown 2015). In India, since the start of the millennium, there has been a concerted effort on the parts of Bollywood producers to make family films capable both of appealing to mass audiences in India, and crossing over to international markets. In the market economy of post-Soviet Russia, locally-produced films must compete with imported Hollywood fare. The animation studio,

Melnitsa, has achieved considerable commercial success and national acclaim in recent years with a series of films based on Russian folklore, but which borrow stylistically from Western (and particularly Disney) animation. Across these various traditions, only the British films, which were aided by Hollywood's distribution machinery, and the French *Asterix* films, distributed by the European mini-major Pathé, have secured a major international market. The popularity of the Indian, Chinese and Russian films has largely been restricted to national audiences.

The withdrawal of state financial support for children's films in several countries does not mean that they are viewed as expedient. In Britain and India, where the pedagogic impulse in children's film has largely been sublimated to pleasure, politicians have continued to emphasise the ongoing need for such films. A 2012 report commissioned by the British government's Department for Culture, Media and Sport argued that the British Film Institute should support the development of films 'for children and their parents or carers' ('A Future for British Film': 39). Similarly, Indian Chief Minister Kiran Kumar Reddy advised the film industry to 'Make films that promote family values' ('Clean Films'). There is clearly still a widespread acceptance in many countries that films for children remain socially desirable, but the less active role of the state reflects a shift away from interventionist models of governance. Mindfulness of the historical (mis) uses of state propaganda in Nazi Germany and Soviet Russia has surely also contributed to the conviction that the state has no business inculcating moral and behavioural values in young children in this way.

The transition from non-commercial children's films to commercial family films is also underpinned by the broad international turn to market economics, and, relatedly, faith in private enterprise to cater to such demand. In some countries where children's film production is at a low level, imported children's films are viewed widely. For instance, as in many countries, Brazilian children mostly watch Hollywood films, despite some faltering attempts at establishing effective local competition (Ou and Constantino Gamo 2015). Although China has a long tradition in the production of children's films, since the 1990s the country has been an especially avid consumer of Hollywood family films. As Ting He notes, Hollywood family entertainment is 'an important part of everyday entertainment for Chinese consumers' in a period where the country's theatrical market has become the second largest in the world (2013: i).

The commercial (and therefore cultural) centrality of Hollywood child-oriented films is examined in more detail in Chapter 2. Chapter 3, by contrast, focuses on twentieth-century children's films that were founded primarily on nationalistic and/or pedagogic grounds, in countries such as Soviet-era Russia, Germany, India, China and Britain. Finally, Chapter 4 examines contemporary, non-Hollywood children's films, and how – increasingly – they operate within transnational industrial and cultural contexts, before drawing some general conclusions about the form in relation to genre, culture and society.

2   HOLLYWOOD, CHILDREN'S CINEMA AND
THE FAMILY AUDIENCE

Hollywood has been the world's most prolific and the most influential producer of children's films since the early days of cinema. *The Wizard of Oz,
E.T.* and the *Harry Potter* series are amongst the most profitable films ever
made, and the products of a single studio – The Walt Disney Company –
have become virtually synonymous, in the minds of many consumers, with
the children's film itself. But it is not merely on account of Hollywood's
pre-eminence that it warrants special consideration. Hollywood represents
the quintessence of children's cinema as a commercial entity. Unlike many
of the films discussed in the next chapter, the aim is neither to educate nor
to instruct, but merely to make money.

Mostly, Hollywood makes 'family films' rather than 'children's films':
they are produced for mixed audiences of children and adults. This has been
the case since the early part of the twentieth century, when Hollywood's
burgeoning studio system extended its distribution network nationally and
internationally. Whilst children were amongst cinema's most enthusiastic
early patrons, producers typically addressed an all-encompassing 'family
audience', envisaging parents and children happily partaking of the same
screen entertainments. Almost without exception, 'children's films' made
in the United States have been exploitation releases produced by minor-
league studios or by independent producers targeting niche audiences.

Addressing the 'family audience' is a matter of commercial pragmatism.
Films capable of attracting a broad cross-section of audiences – appealing to as many and offending as few people as possible – stand the best

chance of returning a profit. However, differentiating between 'children's films' and 'family films' is not just semantic quibbling. In many instances, there are clear lines of demarcation. Films that address adults usually do so through a structured, multi-layered mode of appeal. This chapter will reflect on the child-adult 'doubleness' that is central to the study of children's cinema in general, and child-oriented films in the United States in particular. It will also explore how the production of such films is linked with culture and industry.

Children's Films in Pre-Sound Hollywood

For several reasons, any discussion of 'children's films' or even 'family films' in relation to Hollywood's silent era (circa 1896–1929) is far from straightforward. In this period, the feature film was just one part of a 'balanced programme' of attractions constituting an evening's entertainment at the movie theatre. During the 1920s, movie programmes typically comprised a newsreel, a cartoon, one or more comedy shorts, a live musical interlude and a feature film. At this point, movie-going was one of the dominant social activities in North America, and a weekly visit to the cinema was a way of life for a large percentage of the population. As such, programmes offered a diverse a range of attractions to appeal to the wide cross-section of audiences. The short subjects – especially serials, comedies and, by the mid-1920s, cartoons – were mostly escapist, with particular appeal to children and adolescents, while feature films were more oriented thematically to adult tastes. For this reason, very few features were produced, explicitly, for the consumption of juvenile audiences.

The relative lack of films specifically for children was a matter of intense controversy. The National Board of Review, an influential lobby, called for 'recognition of the fact that most film dramas are made for the consumption of adults' and set up a subsidiary organisation, the National Juvenile Motion Picture League, to campaign for specialised production of children's films (Jowett 1976: 129). Other reformers channelled their energies into setting up 'matinee' programmes for children. Children's matinees were special performances, usually at weekends, where children could view specially tailored programs of shorts and features at a reduced cost. Typically, they were collaborative ventures between theatre managers and interested civic organisations such as PTAs, local boards of education and women's clubs. Content varied, but most matinees were patchworks of lowbrow, but largely unobjectionable, commercial shorts, especially comedies, westerns and serials. There were occasional adaptations of more middlebrow literary classics, and sometimes original 'educational' films, but matinees were always limited by the basic shortfall in material felt to be suitable. Another difficulty was the lack of industry support. Matinees were often unprofitable, and the movement would never have taken off without the sponsorship and persistency of voluntary organisations.

Inevitably, there is a shortage of substantive data upon which to formulate a reliable picture of children's movie-going habits during this period. However, three large-scale studies give an indication. In 1923, the Russell Sage Foundation, the National Board of Review and Associated First National Pictures jointly conducted a nationwide survey of 37,000 thousand high-school students across 76 North American cities (Koszarski 1990: 29). In 1929, Alice Miller Mitchell published a survey of 10,000 Chicago children of varying ages in her book, *Children and Movies*. Finally, Edgar Dale conducted an investigation of the movie attendance habits of young people aged between eight and eighteen in Columbus, Ohio, during the spring of 1929, the results of which were eventually published in 1935 as *Children's Attendance at Motion Pictures*. Although piecemeal, the data assembled from these studies correlate in several key areas. Most boys and girls went to the movies at least once a week, often from a very young age. From adolescence, it became increasingly common for children to attend with friends, rather than with families. Finally, although expressing a preference for particular forms of entertainment – westerns and comedies for boys, and love stories and comedies for girls – pre-teen, adolescent and teenage audiences patronised and enjoyed all kinds of movies.

The films of Mary Pickford, Charlie Chaplin, Harold Lloyd, Tom Mix and Rin Tin Tin were all ideal cross-demographic entertainment, but none of them were produced solely or specifically for children. However, some producers of short films *did* explicitly target younger audiences. The most notable was Hal Roach, whose long-running *Our Gang* (1922–44) series centred on the misadventures of a large, multiracial gang of street children. Another popular format was the serial, which was distinguished by cliff-hangers designed to draw young viewers back week after week. Many serials were comic-book adaptations or westerns, but the primary ingredient was inexpensive action and adventure. Serials emerged at a time when movie audiences were dominated by working-class patrons, and initially, Raymond William Stedman suggests, they were consumed by children and adults alike (1971: 51). Subsequently, serials catered primarily for the cheap, accessible neighbourhood theatres ('nabes'), many of which were frequented in huge numbers by children (Dale 1935: 61). Due to the constant demand from young audiences, the 1910s and 1920s was perhaps the only period in Hollywood's history when feature films for children (as opposed to family films) were produced on a large scale.

Children and Family Audiences in 1930s Hollywood

The transition to sound was a watermark not only in the broader history of Hollywood cinema, but also in the development of specialised family films. 'Talkies' offered much greater potential for 'adult' content and this intensified pressures on Hollywood to reform. Hollywood's trade organisation – the Motion Picture Producers and Distributors of America (MPPDA) – was forced to pre-empt Federal intervention by introducing the Production Code (a.k.a. the 'Hays Code') in April 1930. Written by two prominent Catholics, the Code precluded certain forms of 'adult' content, notably depictions of violence, sexuality, profanity, obscenity, vulgarity and other 'repellent subjects'. However, until 1934, adherence to the Production Code was voluntary, and a succession of adult-oriented film cycles overtook movie screens, including sex comedies and crime films. In early 1934, the Catholic Church – backed by Jewish and Protestant leaders – threatened to boycott the cinema unless effective self-censorship was established. The industry eventually bowed to overwhelming pressure: in July 1934 the Production Code Administration (PCA) was formed, with powers to demand changes to films falling foul of the Code. Theoretically, this meant that all Hollywood productions were 'suitable' for the enjoyment of family audiences, and that children could view them in safety.

However, the proliferation of the 'family film' had less to do with external political pressures or the influence of the Production Code than the commercial imperative to address mass audiences. RKO's *Little Women* (George Cukor, 1933), adapted from Louisa May Alcott's 1869 novel, was a breakthrough film. Many of its attributes – the historical setting, focus on the family, coming-of-age narrative, atmosphere of gentility and the particular appeal for women – formed a successful template for subsequent family-friendly literary adaptations, and, indeed, for many of the most successful family films of the studio era. Crucially, *Little Women* was overly marketed toward adults *as well as* children. The press book emphasised that:

> It hits home to the kids, the grown-ups and the grandfathers and grandmothers. For the street to the school and from the lobby to the last house on the highway its praises will be understood if they are sung.

The fourth highest-grossing film of the decade, *Little Women* led to a series of family-oriented adaptations of literary classics, including *Treasure Island* (Victor Fleming, 1934), *Great Expectations* (Stuart Walker, 1934), *David Copperfield* (Clarence Brown, 1935), *A Midsummer Night's Dream* (Max Reinhardt and William Dieterle, 1935), *Little Lord Fauntleroy* (John Cromwell, 1936), *Romeo and Juliet* (George Cukor, 1936), *Poor Little Rich Girl* (Irving Cummings, 1936), *Captains Courageous* (Victor Fleming, 1937), *The Prisoner of Zenda* (John Cromwell, 1937), *The Adventures of Tom Sawyer* (Norman Taurog, 1938), *The Little Princess* (Walter Lang, 1939) and *The Wizard of Oz*. These films targeted educators and civic and religious reformers as well as parents (Brown 2013b). Rarely did they address children directly: the assumption was that children went to see films selected by, and in the company of, their parents.

The child-star film also reached its pinnacle in the 1930s. Young performers such as Mary Pickford and Jackie Coogan were amongst the most successful stars of the silent era, but the subsequent popularity of Shirley Temple was unparalleled. Having risen to prominence in *Bright Eyes* (David Butler, 1934) at the age of six, Temple became the top box office attraction in US theatres in 1935–38. Her vehicles, like those of fellow child-stars Jane Withers and Deanna Durbin, had a sizable juvenile fan-base, but the child-star film responded primarily to adult concerns. Child stars were loci of emotional uplift during the dark days of the Great Depression. Temple vehicles like *Bright Eyes*, *Our Little Girl* (John S. Robertson, 1935) and *Poor Little Rich Girl* operated almost as licensed public propaganda, addressing adult anxieties regarding economic hardship and fostering hopes of recovery. Appearing as a Rooseveltian figure of optimism, in her films she transforms the lives of a succession of down-at-heel figures through sheer force of goodness. In a well-known but possibly apocryphal 1934 speech tacitly acknowledging her predominantly adult appeal (and utility), President Roosevelt is said to have eulogised: 'It is a splendid thing that for just 15 cents, an American can go to a movie and look at the smiling face of a baby and forget his troubles' (Kasson 2008: 187).

Another foundational film in the development of children's cinema in the United States was released in late 1937 in time for the Christmas family trade. Disney's *Snow White and the Seven Dwarfs* was a hugely profitable and iconic production in its own right, becoming the second highest-grossing film of the decade. But it carried additional significance as Hollywood's first animated feature film, and the first full-length film produced by Disney, the company that became almost synonymous with North American family entertainment from the 1950s onwards. *Snow White* began a long-running trend of appropriating folk tales and fairy tales from other national traditions, bowdlerising them and rebranding them as quintessentially North American entertainments. While adhering fairly closely to its immediate source (the Brothers Grimm's 1812 story 'Snow White'), the film greatly expands on the role of the ingratiatingly adorable dwarfs. Until *The Lion King* (Roger Allers and Rob Minkoff, 1994), and with the partial exception of *Fantasia* (James Algar et al., 1940), all of Disney's animated features were adapted from established source texts, many of them classical fairy tales. Stories were selected on the basis of their congruence with North American values (individualism, paternalism, meritocratic self-advancement), as well as Disney's established brand identity as a purveyor of narratives that promote fun, happiness, friendship, family, justice, and perseverance. Jack Zipes argues that almost all of Disney's fairy tale films exhibit the same essential characteristics:

> The disenfranchised or oppressed heroine must be rescued by a daring prince. Heterosexual happiness and marriage are always the ultimate goals of the story. There is no character development since all figures must be recognisable as character types that remain unchanged throughout the film. Good cannot become evil, nor can evil become good. This world is viewed in Manichean terms as a dichotomy. Only the good will inherit the earth. (Zipes 1995: 110–12)

Innovation, Zipes argues, is largely confined to technical and aesthetic elements, such as 'innovative camera work, improved colour, greater synchronisation, livelier music and lyrics, and unique drawings of exotic characters' (ibid.). Later in this chapter, I will consider the extent to which Zipes's characterisation still holds in relation to contemporary Disney films.

Unquestionably, *Snow White* elevated the status of animation – still largely seen as a lowbrow, child-oriented medium – as a popular art form. At the time of its release, Mrs. William Dick Sporberg, writing in the MPPDA's publication, *The Motion Picture and the Family*, wrote that the film 'may solve for all time the problem of children's pictures', speculating that 'the animated cartoon may be the medium which appeals most strongly to the young people of America' (1937: 3–4). Most critics and exhibitors saw the film's appeal in even broader terms. *The Motion Picture and the Family* was not atypical in its assessment:

> Once in a while there is an event in the motion picture world which may truly be called epochal. Such an occasion was the launching of D. W. Griffith's *Birth of a Nation*. Still another was the memorable evening in 1929 when Al Jolson's voice was briefly heard in *The Jazz Singer* and the era of talking pictures was born. A third has happened the past month with the release of [...] *Snow White and the Seven Dwarfs*. ('Production of Snow White')

Boxoffice magazine concurred, describing *Snow White* as 'the most important picture, from a production perspective, since the advent of sound', and adding that:

> Every man, woman and child who regularly patronises pictures will desire to see it, as will untold thousands who rarely or never attend motion picture theatres; for it has a universal appeal, seldom, if ever before, attained in the realm of celluloid entertainment. (Spear 1937)

Many exhibitors also highlighted the film's universalism. One Nebraskan theatre manager enthused:

> Hats off to Walt Disney. Here is possibly the grandest thing offered to the public for entertainment. It appeals to every living person

from the ages of 2 to 102. After personally viewing this picture sixteen times, I regretted to see it leave the town. (Farrand Thorp 1945: 16)

Contemporary discourses, coupled with the film's enormous box office popularity, thus reaffirm Walt Disney's claim ('we don't think of grown-ups and we don't think of children') that his productions transcended the children's film arena (Merlock Jackson 2006: 13–14).

The Wizard of Oz, even more than Snow White, has come to be seen as the quintessential family film of the classical Hollywood cinema. It employs the children's literary trope of the 'circular journey' – the syuzhet pattern of home-away-home – in Dorothy Gale's (Judy Garland) journey from Kansas to Oz and back to Kansas again at the close of the film. The victory of good over evil (the defeat of the Wicked Witch of the West), the moral lesson ('there's no place like home') and the processes of learning and coming-of-age are also strongly evident; Dorothy's reconciliation to the pleasures and comforts of her outwardly unexciting home life represents her maturation to a more considered, reasoned and pragmatic adult identity. As discussed in Chapter 1, the narrative closure and emotive uplift of the final scenes are prototypical elements of the Hollywood family film (and, indeed, of classical children's literature). The film's cross-demographic narrative appeal is broadened by its use of major adult stars and by its aesthetic richness: vivid Technicolor (cf. Snow White), impressive special effects and musical numbers.

The Wizard of Oz is widely described, alternately, as a 'children's film' and as a 'family film'. We can shed light on this ambivalent generic identity by examining the discourses of promotion and reception that surrounded the film on initial release. The film's press book, produced for distribution to theatre managers throughout the United States, claimed that 'the story has an adult appeal in plot, cleverness in lines and situations, lilting songs which will delight all from 3 to 103, [and] lyrics which will amuse the youngsters and bring chuckles to the grown-ups'. MGM mounted a huge marketing campaign to assert the film's prestige and universal appeal. A two-page ad in Film Daily claimed that '400 happy theatres are about to play it in the largest simultaneous booking of film history' ('Oz'), and listed full-page spreads both in national general-interest publications (such as the Women's Home Companion, Good Housekeeping and Parents'

The restoration of order in the closing stages of *The Wizard of Oz* (1939)

Magazine) and juvenile publications (e.g. *Boys' Life, American Boy* and *American Girl*). Furthermore, MGM, taking its cue from Disney's lucrative partnership with Kay Kamen, launched an unprecedented licensing and commercial drive. 'Several million juvenile and color books' were produced in association with a Wisconsin-based publisher in advance of the film's August 1939 release date ('Juvenile Books'). Moreover, in December 1939, the studio established a new licensing department specifically to exploit *The Wizard of Oz* and its other marquee attraction, *Gone With the Wind* (Victor Fleming, 1939) ('Bagdad').

What, then, do we know about how the film was received? Firstly, it grossed in the region of $2 million. While this constituted an overall loss, this still places it as a major box office hit. It was also nominated for six Academy Awards (including Best Picture), winning two (Best Original Song and Best Original Score). Both *Parents' Magazine* and *Boxoffice* adjudged it the best 'family film' of the month. The *Motion Picture Herald* described it as a film for 'the young at heart', implying an appeal to the internalised 'inner child' ('Showmen's Reviews'). It was reported that adults represented about 60 per cent of patrons in the United Artists theatre, Chicago, despite the expectations of 'circuit executives who thought that children would be the largest part of the audience' ('Campaign Raises'). Of course, the ratio of children and adults in the audience would have depended on several variables, particularly the type and the location of the theatre (whether big city or small town; metropolitan or neighbourhood).

Exhibitors' reports submitted to trade publications offer further insight. One exhibitor from Old Town, Maine, advised: 'Don't listen to what some people say about being a kid's picture. This is one of the biggest kids-adult picture[s] you have ever played' ('What the Picture Did for Me', 23 September 1939). Another, from Ozark, Missouri, reported: 'Not only pleased the children but was very well received from the grownups. The most beautiful picture ever put on the screen to my notion' ('What the Picture Did for Me', 20 January 1940). A manager from Hay Springs, Nebraska, observed that 'it fully satisfied grownups as well as the children' ('What the Picture Did for Me', 23 December 1939). In contrast, one from Dewey, Oklahoma, claimed that 'Business was good, but mostly kids' ('What the Picture Did for Me', 21 October 1939), and an exhibitor from Manassa, Colorado, lamented that 'we had no trouble in selling it to children but just about one-third of our regular adult patrons were not present' ('What the Picture Did for Me', 30 December 1939). Finally, an exhibitor from Lincoln, Kansas dismissively referred to it as 'one of those problem child things that they make' ('What the Picture Did for Me', 4 November 1939). The obvious conclusion from such varied assessments is that, whatever may be present 'in the text' (and this, in part, is a matter of subjective interpretation), popular perceptions of generic identity – most pertinently, the distinctions between 'children's film' and 'family film' – are heavily shaped by contextual discourses and a multiplicity of other external factors. Yet the appeal of such films for adults as well as for children is always clearly apparent.

Children's Shorts and Features

In the age of the balanced programme, the short film was often the domain of children (and of like-minded adults). Slapstick comedies, westerns, serials and cartoon shorts were perennials of the Hollywood short. Of these, the most popular was the cartoon, which came to prominence during the 1920s and remained a vital part of the theatrical package in North America until the 1950s. The cartoon short was far more technically and thematically diverse than might be inferred from a vague familiarity with Disney's features. By the mid-1930s, all of the major Hollywood studios had their own animation divisions, or else held distribution deals with affiliated animation studios. Each studio developed its own recurrent characters and 'house style', particularly after the arrival of synchronous sound and the advent of Technicolor in the early 1930s. For instance, while Disney was known for its hyper-realism, sentiment, overt moralism and cuddliness, (the post-1935) Warner Bros. became associated with irony and comic anarchism.

Many of Disney's 1930s shorts are both unerringly optimistic and unapologetically didactic. Running to approximately seven minutes, they present a diverse range of aesthetic and narrative pleasures, including Technicolor (in what was primarily an age of black and white cinema), high technical quality, relentless cheeriness in tone, the prominence of musical numbers (particularly in the 'Silly Symphonies' series, which ran from 1929–39), gags built on visual incongruities, the presence of anthropomorphised animals, happy endings, the marginalisation or defeat of antagonistic characters or disturbing themes, and a pat moral coda.

The Silly Symphonies series offers straightforward, easily grasped moral homilies. In *The Flying Mouse* (David Hand, 1934), a young mouse longs to be able to fly 'like the birds'. When a fairy grants his wish and gives him bat-like wings, his non-conformity is rejected, in turn, by the birds, by his own family and by the bats. Ultimately, he is transformed back into a mouse and is accepted back into the family home. The film presents a homily on the need to accept your lot in life. (Perhaps there is also a hint of 'sticking to your own', a possible racial overtone deepened by the sinister blackness of the bats.) *The Grasshopper and the Ants* (Wilfred Jackson, 1934) reaffirms hard work and productivity, warning against complacency and indolence. It centres on a carefree grasshopper that refuses to work and spends his time singing and dancing in natural frivolity, contrasting him with a colony of ants which works throughout the summer to prepare for the hardships of winter. Pulling together productively in a common cause in this way insures against future hardships. This message might particularly have chimed for the Depression-era audiences of the mid-1930s. *The Tortoise and the Hare* (Wilfred Jackson, 1935) reminds viewers that slow and steady wins the race, with the honesty and determination of the tortoise ultimately prevailing over the arrogance and ostentation of the hare, who underestimates the need for learned skill and application. Other Disney shorts of the period celebrate such virtues as organisation and industriousness (*Three Little Pigs*, Bill Gillet, 1933), honesty and fair play (*The Pied Piper*, Wilfred Jackson, 1933) and making good on one's obligations towards friends (*The Wise Little Hen*, Wilfred Jackson, 1934).

Although many of Disney's formal innovations (e.g. overlapping action; squash-and-stretch) were widely adopted in the industry, rival studios such as the Fleischer Brothers and Warner Bros. employed other methods of engaging with mass audiences. Many animated shorts operate a familiar child-adult double text, presenting innuendo or political subtexts that may be discerned by mature audiences but will pass largely unnoticed by children. Some cartoons made in the pre-Code era are notably lewd. Betty Boop, the coquettish star of the Fleischer productions, became something of a sex symbol, and in films like *Any Rags?* (Dave Fleischer, 1932) – in which her blouse repeatedly flops down to expose her brassiere – she is overtly sexualised. Warner animator Tex Avery's shorts are similarly 'adult', but in a different way: his films tend towards self-conscious irony, both visual and verbal. The madcap Daffy Duck (a blatant variation on Disney's Donald Duck), for instance, inhabits a Saturnalian world of logical impossibilities, where little truck is given to ingratiating cuteness or sentiment.

Moral lessons are largely absent in the Warner Bros. cartoons, and the 'happy ending' is more ambiguously situated. The rivalry between Bugs Bunny and the gun-toting human hunter, Elmer Fudd, is never definitively resolved (although the death of the rabbit is teased in Chuck Jones's celebrated 1957 short, *What's Opera, Doc?*). Instead, most films conclude with an open-ended maintenance of the status quo. In the first of the Bugs Bunny shorts, *The Wild Hare* (Tex Avery, 1940), the rabbit pretends that Elmer Fudd has succeeded in shooting him, and the hunter collapses remorsefully into flood of tears before marching away, cursing 'rabbits!' and 'carrots!' in equal measure. At this point, Bugs turns directly to the camera and exclaims, 'Can you imagine anybody acting like that? You know, I think the poor guy's screwy'. This narrative technique of crowning an absurd situation with a knowingly self-conscious or fourth-wall-breaking gag becomes a *sine qua non* of the Warner Bros. oeuvre.

Other cartoon shorts were more escapist and action-oriented. MGM's Tom and Jerry series (1940–58) is notably violent, although the anarchic comic destructiveness that Tom and Jerry wreak on each other and their surroundings remains joyous because it is free from consequence. In this cartoon tradition, victims suffer mild inconvenience rather than lasting physical or psychological damage, allowing normal status to be resumed in time for the next film. The Fleischer Brothers' *Superman* series (1941– 43), produced for MGM, more closely ascribes to the conventions of the period's live-action children's films in its uncomplicated action-adventure narratives. Nonetheless, though largely devoid of the *explicit* moralism of the Disney cartoons, they are scarcely lacking in moral undertones. The first film in the series, simply entitled *Superman* (Dave Fleischer, 1940), supplies the necessary victory of good over evil, personified by a stereotypically mad scientist bent on world destruction. In subordinating the female lead, Lois Lane, to the role of naïve ingénue who needs to be rescued, is it strongly patriarchal. Furthermore, as Eric Smoodin points out, these cartoons often concern Superman vanquishing fiendish plots by German and/or Japanese agents (1993: 39–40). As such, these seemingly apolitical cartoons explicitly served as World War II propaganda.

The late 1930s also saw a revitalisation of the live-action serial format, which had fallen precipitously from its peak of popularity in the 1910s ('Serials Making Comeback'). Most serials fell squarely into the B movie category; they were low-risk, low-return ventures and represented themselves overtly – perhaps centrally – as lightweight and disposable. Distinguished by fantastic or action-adventure situations, heavy use of melodrama and exaggerated characterisations, the typical serial comprised about 13 episodes (although some were longer), with an average length of around 20 minutes. Contrary to common assumption, serials were rarely produced exclusively for children (Barefoot 2011), but youngsters were clearly the primary intended audience for such productions as Mascot's *The Phantom Empire* (Otto Brower and B. Reeves Eason, 1935), Universal's *Flash Gordon* (Frederick Stephani, 1936) and *Buck Rogers* (Ford Beebe and Saul A. Goodkind, 1939), and Republic's *Zorro Rides Again* (William Witney and John English, 1937) and *Adventures of Captain Marvel* (Witney and English, 1941). Such productions seldom operated in the contemporary 'adult' world, so were less overtly political. This, too, made them ideal escapist entertainment for contemporary children. Indeed, many serials had a long – if not exactly lucrative – afterlife in children's matinees for many years after their initial release.

Serials produced during World War II, in common with most Hollywood films, had clear propagandist functions. For a modern viewer, their nation-alism – and, in many cases, their racism and xenophobia – is immediately apparent. In Columbia's *Batman* (Lambert Hillyer, 1943; 15 chapters), the DC Comics' antihero is reconstituted as a US government agent protect-ing the country from the threat of fascism. The serial's opening voiceover narration asserts that Batman and Robin 'represent American youth who love their country and are glad to fight for it', adding that 'at this very hour when the Axis criminals are spreading their evil over the world, even within our own land, Batman and Robin stand willing to fight them to the death'. The serial not only upholds the principles of the war, but aims to engender patriotic feeling in its young male audiences in preparation for likely ser-vice in the nation's armed forces. The racist portrayal of the Japanese vil-lains is typical of the period. There are numerous references to 'shifty-eyed Japs', and the criminals' leader, Dr. Daka (played by an orientalised white actor, J. Carrol Naish) is said to receive his dastardly orders direct from the Emperor Hirohito, thus explicitly linking villainy on the home front with the highest levels of Japanese society and state. The serial format survived into the 1950s, but was eventually killed off by the rise of television and by the changing nature of film exhibition, with the 'balanced programme' gradually giving way to single or double features.

While the feature film was largely the preserve of the all-encompassing 'family audience', there was a parallel tradition of inexpensive features tai-lored to child and adolescent consumers during the late 1930s and 1940s. Most such films were produced by so-called 'poverty row' studios like Republic and Monogram, and 'mini-majors' such as Universal and RKO. The *Tarzan* (1932–48) series began at MGM in 1932 as a high-profile, adult-oriented initiative under the auspices of distinguished producer Irving Thalberg. The playful, sexualised relationship between Tarzan (Johnny Weissmuller) and Jane (Maureen O'Sullivan) was gradually reconfigured to one of wholesome domesticity, particularly after they adopt a 'son', Boy (Johnny Sheffield), in *Tarzan Finds a Son!* (1939). When the franchise was taken over by RKO in 1943, it embraced an even more fantastical, comic-book milieu. By *Tarzan's Desert Mystery* (Wilhelm Thiele, 1943), the hero is battling man-eating plants, dinosaurs and giant spiders.

One of the most popular child-oriented series of the period was *Nancy Drew* (1938–39) based on the adventure books of 'Carolyn Keene', and produced by First National. Each film centres on the exploits of a teenage adventuress (played by 15-year-old Bonita Granville). The naturalistic representation of the central child figure contrasts markedly with the cultivated precocity of child-stars such as Shirley Temple and Deanna Durbin. Nancy is independent, resourceful, brave and clearly more formidable than her male sidekick, Ted Nickerson (Frankie Thomas). These films were made in a period where teenage protagonists in mainstream films were often subject to the will of their domineering parents, within tightly-prescribed family units. Here, Nancy is the obvious star. Such films were an escape from the normative Hollywood portrayal of children either as incompetent or dependent on adults. Here, they are represented as self-sufficient young adults; this vision of young adulthood would surely have appealed to young people seeking to graduate from the constraints of childhood.

The Family-Centred Film

Many Hollywood features intended for 'family audiences' centre on the family unit. During the 1930s, most family-centred films were set in small towns and targeted non-metropolitan audiences. *Ah, Wilderness!* (Clarence Brown, 1935), the first major production of this kind, was subtitled 'A Comedy of Recollection', and centres on a quiet family in a pre-industrialised small town at the turn of the century. It also possesses many of the tropes that came to typify Hollywood family films during the studio era: the focus on a large, extended family; the nostalgic depiction of a simple but spiritually rewarding pastoral life; the misadventures of an adolescent protagonist on the cusp of adulthood; the pronounced importance of the parents, especially the father; the fallibility, sexual temptation and first love of the adolescent protagonist; and, ultimately, the transmission of wisdom and experience from father to son.

Ah, Wilderness! was a template for a succession of long-running, cheaply-made family series spanning the late-1930s and early-1940s. Fox produced a series of low-key, earthy comedies centring on the Jones family (1936–40). The first instalment of the Jones (originally Evers) family series, *Every Saturday Night* (James Tinling, 1936), was marketed towards 'the typical average American household' by providing a glimpse of 'how a typical American family lives, what goes on in the home and what the real relationship is between father and children' (*Every Saturday Night* press book). MGM responded with the Hardy family comedies (1937–46), which MGM studio head Louis B. Mayer apparently regarded as his masterpiece (Harmetz 1977: 11). Set in the fictional town of Carvel, the series centred mainly on the teenaged Andy Hardy (Mickey Rooney) learning life lessons from his august father, Judge Hardy (Lewis Stone). These series were predicated on a view of children as not-yet-competent, and their comical vignettes of small-time family life were underpinned by a serious process of moral and behavioural education.

Many of the most successful Hollywood films of the 1940s and early 1950s made the 'nuclear' or 'extended' family the narrative focus. As such, they offered audience identification across a broad demographic span, from young children to grandparents. These films included *Lassie Come Home* (Fred M. Wilcox, 1943), *Meet Me in St. Louis*, *National Velvet* (Clarence Brown, 1945), *The Yearling* (Clarence Brown, 1946), *Life With Father* (Michael Curtiz, 1947), *I Remember Mama* (George Stevens, 1948), *Cheaper by the Dozen* (Walter Lang, 1950), *Father of the Bride* (Minnelli, 1950), *On Moonlight Bay* (Roy Del Ruth, 1951) and *By the Light of the Silvery Moon* (David Butler, 1953). In most of these films, the central family comprises a strong, financially solvent and community-respected father figure, a pragmatic, influential, housewife and a selection of children of varying ages. Unlike most 1930s family films, the modes of address here are differentiated. *Meet Me in St. Louis*, for example, features a full extended family – two parents, a large group of children and a grandparent – co-habiting, and subplots are developed for each of these characters in turn. Such films operate a dual address, aiming to bring families together through a shared exhibition experience. As the trade book for *Meet Me in St. Louis* extolled, '[it] is one of those rare pictures which is everyone's dish, from grandpa to little sister, because that's exactly whom it's about'.

This preoccupation with the family unit recurs throughout Hollywood's studio era (c. 1930–60), and beyond, with the sentimental and nostalgic representations of domestic life in hugely popular 1960s films, such as *Mary Poppins* (Robert Stevenson, 1964) and *The Sound of Music*. But by the 1970s there was a growing acceptance that family life may be stultifying and dysfunctional, not nurturing and supportive. *The Godfather* (Francis Ford Coppola, 1972) and *Paper Moon* (Peter Bogdanovich, 1973), two of the most popular family-life films of the decade, were cynical and adult-oriented. Similarly, Steven Spielberg's family-oriented films, *Close*

The primacy of the nuclear family in *Mary Poppins* (1964)

Encounters of the Third Kind (1977) and *E.T. The Extra-Terrestrial*, represent the family unit as a potential site of conflict and instability. In both films, the *paterfamilias* abandons his family in search of personal fulfilment, and in *E.T.* the effects of this decision on the rest of the family is explored in some depth: the children are seen glumly lamenting their father's absence, and the matriarch teeters on the brink of a nervous breakdown. Growing acceptance of changing family structures and the rising divorce rates in the United States is reflected in *Mrs. Doubtfire*. Released more than a decade after *E.T.*, the film is able to posit a more hopeful future for 'family' *after* the divorce of the parents. The increasing normalisation of the single-parent family is acknowledged in *Toy Story*, where the absence of the patriarch in context of a single-parent household – whether due to death, divorce, separation or surrogacy – is never explicitly commented on.

Ideas of family remain intrinsic to the Hollywood child-oriented film. Even in films such as *E.T.* and *Mrs. Doubtfire* where the 'traditional' nuclear family has fragmented, family endures in different configurations. The presence of the benign alien in *E.T.* seems to offer emotional healing to the remaining members of a broken family. The love, support and interde-pendency implicit in the relationship between the children and the alien also fulfil many of the most important functions of family life. This notion of symbolic family is increasingly important in Hollywood cinema. In *Toy Story*, the anthropomorphised toys view themselves not just as playthings but as surrogate parents for the fatherless human child. In many other films, from *The Wizard of Oz* to more recent productions such as *Monsters, Inc.* (Pete Docter, 2001), friendship and family are bound together. In the absence of literal representations of the (human) domestic environment, family is an institution of learning and mutual support rather than a rigidly patriarchal system based exclusively on blood ties and hierarchies of power. In such films, the spectator might relate these literal and symbolic families to their own life experiences, but their presence also serves as a utopian reminder that family, in whatever form, will endure.

Hollywood and Family Entertainment 1950–1975

Until the 1950s, Disney was not widely considered to be the leading purveyor of family entertainment in Hollywood. When *Parents' Magazine* honoured a famous studio head in 1949 with a special award for the company that had produced the 'greatest list of family pix', the recipient was not Walt Disney, but MGM's Louis B. Mayer ('Mayer, Schary, Rodgers'). MGM was also awarded a citation by *Boxoffice* in 1953 for having produced the greatest quantity of family films since 1932 ('MGM Wins Most Blue Ribbons'). There were five key factors in Disney's ascendance to its almost monolithic status in the family entertainment business: i) the popularity of its live-action production wing, starting with *Treasure Island* (Byron Haskin, 1950); ii) the creation of its own distribution arm, Buena Vista, in 1953, removing its prior dependence on rival studio RKO to distribute its films; iii) its pioneering partnership with television network ABC in 1954, in which the network offered investment in return for an exclusive television show (*Walt Disney's Disneyland*, 1954–58) and other original material; iv) the release of its live-action spectacular *20,000 Leagues Under the Sea* (Richard Fleischer, 1954), which addressed an older adolescent-teenage audience; and v) the opening of theme park Disneyland in 1955, which was partly funded by the ABC deal. Disneyland was immediately successful: in 1956, its first year of business, it received about three million visitors; over the next decade, this figure rose to nearly seven million (Schickel 1997: 19, 36). Furthermore, reputedly more than three-quarters of park attendees were teenagers or adults (Merlock Jackson 2006: 89–103). Disney's success during this period reflects its expansion into alternative revenue streams. The firm was no longer simply an animation studio, nor a producer of 'children's films', but a diversified multimedia conglomerate. Other Hollywood studios, attempting to differentiate their product from television, exploited censorship liberalisation to produce edgy, often violent and sexualised films for the 'adult' and 'youth' demographics. Otto Preminger's *The Moon is Blue* (1953) was the first major studio production released without a seal of approval from the PCA. Preminger's *The Man with the Golden Arm* (1955) and Elia Kazan's *Baby Doll* (1956) were similarly controversial, receiving 'Condemned' ratings from the Catholic Legion of Decency. The trend continued to the extent that, by 1966, only 59 per cent of films released in the United States were approved by the PCA as being suitable for family audiences (Farber 1972: 12). The huge popularity of *Rock Around the Clock* (Fred F. Sears, 1956), the prototypical rock 'n' roll film, proved 'that teenagers alone could sustain a box-office hit' (Doherty 2002: 57). By the 1960s, US network television, with its in-built national audience, had effectively colonised the 'family' market. Even Disney's theatrical releases increasingly missed their mark. Indeed, *The Jungle Book* (Wolfgang Reitherman, 1967) and *The Love Bug* (Robert Stevenson, 1968) were Disney's last major box office hits until the late 1980s.

The Family Film and Children's Media in Contemporary Hollywood

The latter-day structural centrality of the family film can be traced back to the late-1970s Hollywood blockbuster. George Lucas's *Star Wars*, Steven Spielberg's *Close Encounters of the Third Kind* (1978), and Warner Bros.' *Superman* (Richard Donner, 1978) represented a new type of family film that Peter Krämer has termed the 'family-adventure movie'. Previously, 'children's films' had been a marginal presence in Hollywood cinema. But as Krämer argues, since the late 1970s most of Hollywood's biggest hits are 'children's films for the whole family and for teenagers, too' (Krämer 2004: 366– 67). *Star Wars* and *E.T.*, in particular, mobilised the now-vital teenage and young adult demographics. Repackaging the unpretentious action-adventure of the cheap 'poverty row' serials of the 1930s and 1940s within a blockbuster aesthetic that drew on new technological potentialities, they also retained the emotive qualities of classical Hollywood family films. But while implicit didactic elements are still present, the overt moralism of films such as *The Wizard of Oz* and the classical-era Disney features is routinely downplayed.

These films are distinguished from earlier family films by their largely undifferentiated modes of address. That is to say, they do not address notional child and adult spectators as separate entities, but rather assume, as Walt Disney did, that audiences of *all ages* may be engaged by similar, but specific, patterns of fantasy. By the early 1980s, the dual-addressed family film of the classical Hollywood had largely been supplanted by the New Hollywood family-adventure movie. Examples include the *Star Wars*, *Superman*, *Star Trek* (1978–) and *Indiana Jones* series, *Ghostbusters* (Ivan Reitman, 1984), *Back to the Future* (Robert Zemeckis, 1985), *Batman* (Tim Burton, 1989), *Jurassic Park* (Steven Spielberg, 1993), *Independence Day* (Roland Emmerich, 1996), and the *Harry Potter, Lord of the Rings, Spider-Man* (2002–), *Chronicles of Narnia* (2005–), *Marvel Cinematic Universe* (2008–) and *Avatar* (2009–) series. These films are components in larger multimedia franchises; they may produce several sequels, but equally important is the scope for 'ancillary' revenues: licensing, merchandising (e.g. toys, clothes, books, games), pay-TV sales and home video. Before *Star Wars*, film licensing rights were often given away for free publicity. Afterwards, as David A. Cook explains, 'merchandising became an industry unto itself, and tie-in product marketing began to drive the conception and selling of motion picture products rather than vice versa' (Cook 2000: 51). During the 1980s, Hollywood studios started to recognise that blockbuster family films, besides their considerable box office potential, also represent the best opportunities for exploiting entertainment across multiple platforms.

The structural centrality of family entertainment is closely linked with the processes of multimedia conglomeration that took place in Hollywood in the 1980s and 1990s, when all of the major Hollywood studios, except Disney, were either acquired by larger multinational corporations or merged with other media companies. In 1985, Turner Broadcasting purchased MGM and News Corporation acquired Twentieth Century-Fox. In 1982, Columbia was bought by Coca-Cola, which then re-sold to Sony in 1989. The same year, Warner Bros. merged with Time-Life to form Time-Warner. In 1990, Universal was acquired by Matsushita Electric, and then sold to Seagram, which in turn sold to Vivendi; since 2004, the firm has been owned by General Electric. In 1993, Viacom acquired Paramount. Among the 'classical' Hollywood majors, only Disney has resisted takeover. This is due, in part, to the fact that its expansion and diversification has always been based on the 'family' entertainment model, a fact demonstrated in recent years by its acquisition of animation studio Pixar in 2006, comic book publisher Marvel in 2009, and production studio LucasFilm (owner of the *Star Wars* franchise) in 2012. It is no coincidence that these media mergers coincided with an upsurge in broad-appeal, family-suitable films, with franchise potential, that could be realised across multiple media platforms. Contemporary Hollywood family entertainment can be understood as the *material* manifestation of a broader universalistic agenda; international conglomeration, expansionism and synergy are the equivalent *corporate* manifestations: they are two sides of the same coin.

Time-Warner was the first major Hollywood studio to announce plans to create a 'family film' production division. This announcement (in December 1991) aroused very little surprise in the industry or the trade press: *Variety* observed that it reflected 'industry-wide awareness that survival in the 1990s may be a matter of creating wholesome, family-oriented entertainment' ('New Plan'). An April 1993 article in *Entertainment Weekly* cited a recent report by entertainment research firm Paul Kagan Associates that advocated greater production of family films, noting that almost half of the 46 movies that grossed in excess of $100 million between 1984 and 1991 were rated 'PG' (Murphy 1993). Over the course of the 1990s, Warner Bros. ('Warner Bros. Family Entertainment'), Twentieth Century-Fox ('Fox Family Films'), Miramax ('Miramax Family Films'), MGM ('MGM/UA Family Entertainment'), Universal ('Universal Family & Home Entertainment'), Viacom ('Nickelodeon Movies') and Sony ('Sony Pictures Family Entertainment Group') created specialised 'family' divisions oriented to the production and multimedia exploitation of live-action and animated films. Since then, new studios – including Pixar, DreamWorks, Laika, Blue Sky Studios and Illumination Entertainment – have joined Disney in the business of producing theatrically-released, feature-length animation for family audiences.

Change and Continuity

By this point, it should be clear why Hollywood cinema warrants particular consideration in a broader overview of children's cinema. North America is the only country in which children's films (or family films) have always been part of the cinematic and cultural mainstream, and in which the commercial, non-pedagogic impulse is far stronger than the didactic imperative that has underpinned children's cinema in the majority of countries. It is also the only country that has successfully exported its child-oriented films to a mass global audience. But to what extent have social and industrial changes affected the form itself? In many regards, there have been significant changes in Hollywood family films since the 1990s. Some of these changes are formal (e.g. the development of CGI, the re-emergence of 3-D, the generic primacy of fantasy) and some are ideological (e.g. liberalising attitudes to race, gender and sexuality). The technological barriers between live-action and animated Hollywood family films have eroded, with 'live-action' films routinely employing computer-generated effects, and the proliferation of digital technologies (such as performance capture) in films of all types. Standards of acceptability have also changed. While most feature animation is currently rated 'U' or 'PG' by the Motion Picture Association of America (MPAA) – ratings that denote suitability for younger children – the majority of live-action family blockbusters are now classified as 'PG-13', which cautions that 'Some material may be inappropriate for children under 13'.

The definition of 'family film' has expanded. It still encompasses more 'traditional' forms, such as cel animation, and familiar genres such as domestic comedy, fairy tale and literary adaptation. But it has also widened to include computer-generated animation, live-action/animation hybrids, fantasy, and blockbuster superhero films pitched at older children, teenagers and adults. This differentiation reflects industry recognition that the 'family audience' is inherently pluralistic, and that consumers – divided by gender, age, class, ethnicity, sexual orientation, and local, regional and national identity – may derive pleasure from different patterns of fantasy. The feature-length animation produced by Disney, Pixar and DreamWorks is aimed at a slightly younger demographic (while remaining hugely popular with older audiences), and most such films are rated 'U' or 'PG'. They are more explicitly moralistic than family-adventure movies such as the *Star Wars* or *Star Trek* series, which tend to be rated 'PG-13' and target adolescents, teenagers and young adults. Some films marketed towards children – such as the *Transformers* series (2007–), which has been advertised during broadcasts of children's shows on US television (Smith 2008) – may not instantly be recognisable as family films, residing on the borderline between 'child' and 'adult' suitability. The 'darkness' and moral ambiguity of the later instalments in Warner Bros.' *Harry Potter* franchise has widely been observed, with directors Mike Newell and David Yates both explicitly stating that their own films in the series were unsuitable for younger children (Gritton 2005; Lawrence 2009). Films have also become longer, on average, belying the old presumption that entertainment for children needs to accommodate their shorter attention spans.

Despite all of this, there are recurrent features that continue to link contemporary family films with studio-era productions. We need to weigh continuities against changes. In this context, it is worth considering two recent, hugely popular, Disney productions: the CGI animation *Frozen* and the primarily live-action feature *Maleficent* (Robert Stromberg, 2014). *Frozen*, Disney's 53rd feature-length animation (and its sixth wholly computer-animated feature), is loosely adapted from Hans Christian Andersen's fairy tale, 'The Snow Queen' (1844), while *Maleficent* is loosely adapted from Charles Perrault's 'Sleeping Beauty' (1697). Besides their considerable international popularity on theatrical release (*Frozen* grossed in excess of $1.2 billion; *Maleficent* more than $750 million), what links these films is their radical reinterpretation of aspects of the source texts. In both cases, the film's co-protagonist is a sympathetic revision of the original story's villainous female, with additional nuances of characterisation. And in both films the primary villain is a duplicitous male figure not present in the source text. This revisionism may have a pragmatic commercial basis: these films, in contrast to the majority of male-oriented family-adventure movies, are intended for girls (and their parents) more than boys. But it is also explicitly, and self-avowedly, political; a determined movement away from the dyadic representations of 'good' and 'bad' femininity that has long bedevilled children's fiction.

In *Frozen* and *Maleficent*, the female protagonists are freed from a reliance on romantic love in order to achieve personal (or social) fulfilment. A conventional, heterosexual romantic coupling is teased, but ultimately disavowed when the man set up as the hero betrays the central female character. While the consequences of these betrayals are still devastating for its victims, the key relationship in both films is between two women: sisters (*Frozen*) and mother and daughter (*Maleficent*). In both films, an act of pure, selfless love from the putatively villainous female restores the stereotypically 'good' princess to health. This family bond is seen to be at

A celebration of sisterly love in *Frozen* (2013)

least equal, if not superior, to the intimacy and transformative power of romantic union. The implication of these acts of revision is twofold. Firstly, women are seen to be sufficiently empowered and self-sufficient not to require a man in their life. Secondly, while heterosexual romance might still be a fulfilling choice for many, it may not (or *need not*) be 'happily ever after'. This deconstructive impulse allegorises current social trends (the normalcy of divorce and/or alternative family structures) and self-reflexively debunks conventions – of courtship, romance and marriage – that have become too clichéd or outmoded to be presented in the earnest, uncynical and politically regressive manner of previous Disney fairy tale films.

These releases may be seen in context of a broader, still incipient, project of liberalisation in Hollywood family films in relation to gender, class, race and sexuality. The self-reliance of the female protagonists in *Frozen* and *Maleficent* can distantly be traced back to the surface non-conformism of 1990s Disney heroines such as Belle in *Beauty and the Beast* (Gary Trousdale and Kirk Wise, 1991). Class is often under-addressed in analyses of family films, but it is notable that both *Frozen* and *Maleficent* equate class hierarchy with corruption and abuse of power. As such, the films are closer to the folkloric roots of fairy tale – which often centres on subaltern sections of society – than to the valorisation of the ruling classes and the trappings of wealth and power of the early Disney features. The seemingly handsome, heroic prince in *Frozen* is a tyrannical despot, and it is the obsessive pursuit of self-advancement that corrupts the peasant boy-turned-king in *Maleficent*. But it is too early to suggest that such portrayals are part of a wider trend. The same is true of the representation of sexual minorities. The underrepresentation of homosexual, bisexual and trans-sexual characters in Hollywood cinema is a widely-observed phenomenon. The comedic revelation in the final scene of the animated family-horror film, *ParaNorman* (Chris Butler and Sam Fell, 2012), that a hyper-masculine young man is gay, and the barely glimpsed, sexually ambiguous female couple in *Finding Dory* (Andrew Stanton and Angus MacLane, 2016), are notable, but isolated, exceptions.

Race is altogether more visible, both in terms of presence and absence. The recasting of the young female protagonist in the remake of *Annie* (Will Gluck, 2014) as a black girl met with support and opprobrium in equal measure. Indeed, that such casting is still controversial in the multiracial context of twenty-first century US society bespeaks the ideological narrow-ness of the Hollywood system. The idealistic, multiracial group dynamic in Hal Roach's *Our Gang* shorts of the 1920s and 1930s is very much an excep-tion within the wider tradition of Hollywood family films. When non-white (and particularly African-American) characters have appeared in Hollywood family films, it has usually been in subordinate positions, or, alternatively, as an exotic 'other', as with Bill 'Bojangles' Robinson's cameos in several Shirley Temple films, or the Indian child-star Sabu during the 1940s. Many of the child-oriented serials of the studio era (especially those produced during wartime) featured 'blacked-up' white actors in villainous roles. The first major family film produced in the United States that centred on a black family, *Sounder* (Martin Ritt, 1972), was produced *outside* of the Hollywood system by an independent producer, Robert B. Radnitz, an outspoken lib-eral who had to battle hard to get his film distributed (Wilson 1994).

It may be tempting, in light of representational and industrial changes, to assume that contemporary Hollywood family films are an altogether dif-ferent entity to classical Hollywood iterations. Certainly, it is always more interesting to argue that innovation trumps convention. But to do so would be to ignore the many commonalities that underpin the genre from its beginnings through to the present day. Despite its twenty-first century atti-tudes towards gender norms, *Frozen* shares numerous characteristics with *Snow White* and *The Wizard of Oz*: the prominence of song-and-dance; the home-away-home syuzhet structure; the provision of narrative closure; the victory of good over evil (even if these moral extremes are initially rendered problematic in the latter's film's protagonist); and strategies of emotional uplift, culminating in the proverbial 'happy ending'. More broadly, these films' use of spectacle, adult stars and nostalgia for childhood are discernible in silent-era family films, such as Mary Pickford's children's literary adaptation vehicles of the 1910s and 1920s. There is an even longer (pre-filmic) tradition of child-centred narratives that operate within fantastic or magical frameworks or a domestic setting, and of moral fables that evoke comfort and reassurance, and reaffirm kinship ties. Finally – and like the films examined in Chapter 3 – all such productions remain bound by social and cultural constructions of childhood that regulate standards of acceptability.

3   CHILDREN'S FILM, NATION AND IDENTITY

Since the early part of the twentieth century, a large percentage of non-Hollywood children's films have been made under the auspices of the nation-state, either by state-funded independent studios or under total systems of state control. The first half of this chapter explores the institutional and ideological commonalities that underpin state-funded children's cinema, and relates them to the wider conventions of children's cinema. The second half goes on to consider how nation and identity are represented in three commercial children's films of the twentieth century.

State-regulated children's cinema is particularly associated with the ideological mission of the Soviet Union and its satellites. In Soviet Russia, children's cinema was an organ of the state ideological machinery from the early 1920s until shortly prior to the collapse of the Soviet Union in 1991. State interest in children's cinema peaked in the 1930s, when the government built special, tax-exempt theatres for child audiences and apportioned 30 per cent of its cinema budget to the production of films for children. As we have seen, in June 1936, *Soiuzdetfilm* and *Soiuzmul'tfilm* were established, and other state-run studios also produced children's films throughout the Soviet era. In the Soviet-controlled German Democratic Republic (GDR, or East Germany), children's cinema was the province of the state-run film production company, DEFA, from 1946 to 1992. In East Germany, unlike in Soviet Russia, child and adult audiences were not separated through the provision of specialised children's theatres. Consequently, DEFA films were consumed by adults as well as children, and the category of 'children's films', separate from 'general audience' films, was a matter of dispute (Blessing 2015: 155). In Czechoslovakia, children's cinema emerged after the post-war nationalisation of the Czech film industry and the founding of Czechoslovak State Film. Whereas both live-action and animated films predominated in Russia and East Germany, in Czechoslovakia animation – particularly puppet animation – was the dominant form; indeed, as Lukáš Skupa observes, it quickly became the international 'showcase' for Czech cinema (2015: 205).

In Britain and India, institutionalised children's cinema emerged from a milder form of socialist interventionism. As noted in Chapter 1, in Britain it was first instituted as an independent enterprise by the movie mogul J. Arthur Rank, whose Children's Entertainment Films (CEF) produced shorts and features for children's matinee exhibition between 1943 and 1950. From 1951 until 1985, the state-backed Children's Film Foundation (CFF) continued to produce films for Saturday morning children's cinema clubs. In India, children's films have been produced on an ongoing basis by the Children's Film Society, India (CFSI) since 1955. Operating under the auspices of the Ministry of Information and Broadcasting, the CFSI survived the country's post-socialist economic liberalisation of the early 1990s, and continues to produce shorts and documentaries in multiple languages. In China, state-supported production of children's films has been ongoing since the founding of the People's Republic in 1949. The Chinese government has sponsored several animation studios, notably the Shanghai Animation Film Studio, established in 1957. Since 1981, it has also put its weight behind the China Children's Film Studio (CCFS), which produces both live-action and animated films. It is estimated that around 400 children's films have been produced with state support in China since 1949 (Ting He 2013: 67–69).

While it is not possible to examine these various traditions in great depth here, several commonalities between them can be adduced. First, and most obvious, is at the organisational level. These children's cinemas have all operated within a centralised, top-down model of popular culture. In such a system, the responsibility for educating and entertaining young people is assumed by the state. Funding comes, directly or indirectly, from state coffers (or, in Britain's case, through a tax levied by the film industry on behalf of the state). The overall level of funding is relatively low compared with mainstream commercial production, a fact that has often reflected trade restrictions on the entry of more lavish foreign films (particularly those produced in Hollywood) rather than a disregard for the importance of the genre. Indeed, in each case, the provision of children's cinema in these countries has been seen as a necessary part of the sociali-sation process.

This leads to the second commonality, which is more political. These traditions of children's cinema were (or still are) produced in communist or socialist systems of government. The overriding motivation is paternalis-tic; none of the resultant films are produced primarily to entertain. Rather, they are instruments of moral and behavioural instruction, and are linked by an understanding of the audience as impressionable, uneducated, and requiring moral guidance. J. Arthur Rank's intention in Britain was to make films that 'do [children] good' (Staples 1997: 91). Such a phrase is doubly loaded. On one level, it registers pedagogic and ethical value. More deeply, as in all of these attempts at mass education, film is seen within a cause-and-effect, hypodermic model of popular culture. While Rank's initiative was putatively philanthropic, it shares with these other programs a mis-trust of the masses and a belief in film's potentiality as a socialising appa-ratus. As Alexander Prokhorev argues, the 'infantilisation of the masses' in the Soviet system 'was part and parcel of the regime's myth of the future utopia', and Soviet children's cinema therefore 'articulated the ideal community of the future as a land of children with the government as the people's authoritarian father' (2008: 129). Similarly, in 1984, Hrishikesh Mukherjee, recently retired chairman of the government-appointed Indian film censorship board, argued that 'audiences are still very immature', and so decisions to censor movie content had 'to take into consideration their receptivity' to potentially corrupting material (Pendakur 1996: 155).

It might be assumed that films produced under such conditions are characterised by a dull uniformity, in which principles of artistry are deci-sively subordinated to those of ideological instruction. However, in most cases this is untrue, and typically filmmakers have retained high degrees of autonomy. Te Wei, the long-standing director of the state-funded Shanghai Animation Film Studio, has recounted his belief that the Chinese government did not interfere in the filmmaking process, because to do so would have inhibited the development of the medium; critic Chen Jianyu adds that: 'The government gave money and collected all the outstanding animators together. How long they took to produce, no one cared' (Lent and Xu 2010: 118). During the 1950s and most of the 1960s, the state-controlled Czech cinema was internationally lauded for its artistry and freedom of expression. Benita Blessing suggests that DEFA producers were also afforded a considerable amount of 'artistic leeway' (2015: 156). Of course, this was not always the case. At times of political instability, such as during World War II, the Chinese Cultural Revolution of the 1960s and 1970s, or the Prague Spring of 1968, the state has taken a more active role, often in ways that circumscribe artistic expression. But even in these instances, state-supported children's cinema has continued to evince a formal and generic pluralism. Films have covered a broad array of styles and a diverse range of genres, including poetic realism, political drama, war films, comedy, musical, biopic, science-fiction, fantasy and fairy tale.

Fairy tale, in particular, has occupied a central position in European traditions of children's cinema. In the United States, fairy tale films are viewed almost as synonymous with Disney, and in Britain and several other countries the genre is largely undeveloped. However, fairy tale adaptations constitute a high percentage of the children's films of Soviet Russia, Czechoslovakia, Germany and Poland, with lesser but still substantial traditions in France, Scandinavia, China, Japan and numerous other countries. This predominance is partly attributable to its instrumental functions. As Jack Zipes observes, 'fairy tales constitute the most profound articulation of the human struggle to form and maintain a civilising process' (2011: 1). Furthermore, many films, such as those made in Germany by Lotte Reiniger and in Russia by Ivan Ivanov-Vano, centre on subaltern sections of society and articulate utopian ideals of freedom and egalitarianism. Their appeal in socialist nations is self-evident. As Prokhorev observes of Soviet Russia, 'fairy tale became the legitimate film genre because it helped to visualise Stalinist culture's spirit of miraculous reality' (2008: 135–36). In Czechoslovakia, fairy tale films had constituted only a small percentage of animated production until around 1950, when the government instructed studios to produce children's films in the belief that young citizens needed to be 'ideologically re-educated' (Skupa 2015: 213–14). Fairy tale film was thus a predominant medium for state propaganda. However, as Zipes argues, fairy tales also enabled politically subversive commentary to be disguised through symbol and allegory (2011: 332).

In either case, fairy tale films reflected a mid-twentieth century tendency towards non-realist modes of artistic discourse. One can perceive aesthetic parallels between Reiniger's silhouette paper animation and the German Expressionist film movement of the 1920s, both of which are far removed from contemporary Anglo-American values of 'realism'. And while early British and North American children's films owed much to Victorian-era children's fiction, traditional folk and fairy tales have played a much larger part in the cultural upbringing of children in continental Europe. The allegorical dimensions of such source texts have perhaps also contributed to the symbolic, non-realist, and often theatrical modes of representation in the fairy tale film, which encompasses live-action, hybrids of live-action and cel animation, puppet animation, stop-motion and paper animation.

Despite this generic pluralism, across state-supported children's cinema as a whole there are several narrative, stylistic and ideological commonalities. Firstly, there is an abiding focus on individual children or groups of children. Accordingly, there is less emphasis on adult characters as symbolic children (in the Laurel and Hardy mode) than in commercial cinema, where the presence of adult stars is seen as necessary to attract a wider audience. As such, there is greater division between (social constructions of) childhood and adulthood, alongside a focus on processes of learning and maturation that child protagonists typically undergo over the course of the narrative. A persistent feature is a valorisation of state and society, and of established structures of social stratification (particularly in terms of class, gender and race). Most films also attempt to instil respect for authority in its many forms. Accordingly, the importance and the sanctity of law and order are reasserted, with criminal elements suitably punished as an example to prospective wrongdoers.

In the Soviet films, structures of power are represented more ambivalently. The authority of the social collective is seen to be absolute; this is an important facet to films that are facilitated by, and ultimately in the service of, the state. But individual rulers, such as aristocrats or tsars, are commonly portrayed as despots or buffoons. This representational trope accorded with Soviet ideology, which placed collective authority over individual action. Similarly, while in most children's films family is a vital agent of socialisation, in the early Soviet films the symbolic family, represented by the state ('Thank You, Comrade Stalin, for Our Happy Childhood!'), has primacy over the biological family. Finally, and relatedly, the vast majority of these films endorse a form of collectivism, not individualism. This is a key distinction from Hollywood cinema, which has followed a prevailing tenet of North

American ideology in valorising the action and presumptive primacy of the individual. The Soviet distrust of the nuclear family is manifest in numerous films in which villainous parents or guardians are unmasked and defeated by patriotic children in deference to the social collective. This negation of the biological family is exceptional in that it is largely confined to Soviet cinema. However, the broader premise of members of the state uniting in a common cause is highly representative of socialist iterations of children's film.

All of these traditions attempt to embody the culture and values of the nation. Indeed, this is the primary reason for the existence of state-supported children's cinema. A major element, of course, is implicit and explicit endorsement of state ideology. But there is also a broader empha-sis on cultural heritage. Such films typically reflect a desire to build on indigenous folkloric, literary and artistic influences, or else to colonise, through strategic revision, the imported culture of other nations. Jack Zipes has remarked on the 'conservative aesthetic designs' of the post-war Soviet animated films, which were indebted to the rounded character design and realism of Disney's animation (2011: 90). Similarly, Soviet animation was heavily reliant on rotoscoping, a cost-cutting technique pioneered by the Hollywood-based Fleischer brothers wherein animators trace the filmed movements of real actors projected on to celluloid. Stalinist children's cinema also drew liberally on Western texts, reconfiguring aspects of the source narratives 'to fit the Marxist theory of class struggle' (Prokhorev 2008: 137). However, Marina Balina and Birgit Beumers also note the artis-tic influence of Russian painters, such as Viktor Vasnetsov, and illustrators, such as Ivan Bilibin (2016: 132). Equally, they argue that the radicalism of these films is located more within its Soviet ideologies of 'class mobility, women's emancipation and empowerment, and the toppling of rulers' than in the specificities of its formal composition.

The Brothers Grimm, not surprisingly, were an abiding source of stories for East German fairy tales. In drawing on these texts, DEFA films could be seen to build on the nation's cultural heritage. However, as with the Soviet filmmakers, DEFA also adapted texts from international folkloric traditions, such as Mongolian and Arabian folk tales and fairy tales (Zipes 2011: 342). Czech filmmakers, too, drew on the work of indigenous writers and collec-tors of folk and fairy tales, such as Alois Jirásek, Karel Erben and Božena Nemcová. *Old Czech Legends* (*Staré pověsti české*, 1953) – produced by the renowned animator Jiří Trnka at the behest of the Czech government – is notable both for the national provenance of its source texts and its fore-grounding of traditional Czech folk music on the soundtrack. Yet Czech stu-dios also adapted works by the Brothers Grimm, Hans Christian Andersen and Charles Perrault. These transnational borrowings do not necessarily connote a shared cultural imaginary, but rather a source bank of broadly intelligible stories that may be repurposed by the coloniser.

Disney has appropriated fairy tales from multiple local and national traditions, rewriting the social and cultural resonances of the source text to accord with the perceived requirements of its audiences. But this cultural appropriation is a two-way process. Trnka adapted Hans Christian Andersen's *The Emperor's Nightingale* (*Císařův slavík*, 1949) and Shakespeare's *A Midsummer Night's Dream* (*Sen noci svatojánské*, 1959) as three-dimensional puppet films. Many Soviet retellings of Western tales (by the likes of Jules Verne and Robert Louis Stevenson) retain the basic plot and narrative structure of the source text, but radically reinter-pret the political and ideological meanings. In Gorky's Stalinist adapta-tion of *Treasure Island* (*Ostrov sokrovishch*, Vladimir Vaynshtok, 1938), for instance, most of the characters and situations are carried over from Stevenson's novel, but it is Irish republicans, not pirates, that are pursuing the treasure in order to fund their rebellion against British imperialism. Here, the Irish nationalists are clearly equated with the Russian revolution-aries that overthrew the Imperial Government.

At times, the popularity of imported cultural products has inhibited the development of indigenous narrative and aesthetic modes. In China, as John A. Lent and Ying Xu suggest, there has been a determined movement to utilise stories from local literature, folklore and proverb (2010: 116). Ting He notes that many of the films of the Shanghai Animation Film Studio are made using traditional methods of painting and paper cutting, and 'look very much like the characters that would appear in a traditional Chinese New Year Painting' (2013: 70). However, for much of its history, Chinese animation has struggled to develop a distinct formal style, firstly from Disney animation (during the 1930s), then from Soviet animation (during the 1950s), and latterly from Japanese anime.

Even under the tighter ideological constraints in state systems such as Soviet Russia and the PRC, considerable variation exists in political expres-sion across the sphere of state-supported children's cinema. Very broadly, films may be divided into three categories in relation to the state system:

- those unambiguously manufactured for purposes of propaganda;
- those that are not explicitly propagandist, but that nevertheless strongly reflect prevailing national concerns and clearly uphold common beliefs;
- and those that, by contrast, are more ambiguously situated in relation to the socio-political status quo, and may articulate degrees of resistance.

The first category is the most clear-cut. State-sanctioned propaganda films aimed at children and young people have been produced, at some point, in most countries. The obvious inference is that such films must be products of totalitarian regimes. However, in periods of ideological conflict – particularly during wartime – they have been made in democratic nations as well, including the United States and Britain. Disney, for instance, made a series of fiction and non-fiction anti-Nazi propaganda films at the behest of the US government during World War II.

There were notable film propaganda movements in Soviet Russia, China and Japan during the same period. In Russia, many wartime films centred on 'young hero martyrs sacrificing their lives in the fight against Nazis' (Prokhorev 2008: 139–40). The Chinese animation pioneers, the Wan Brothers, made a series of anti-Japanese shorts with the support of the state-run China Film Studios during the Japanese occupation (Lent and Xu 2010: 114). Conversely, in Japan, numerous films were constituted as explicit ideological assaults on the United States. For instance, in the animated short, *Momotarō's Sea Eagles* (*Momotarō no Umiwashi*, Mitsuyo Seo, 1943) – produced in collaboration with the Japanese Navy – a character from Japanese folklore, *Momotarō* (literally 'peach boy', because he was born inside a giant peach), leads an attack on 'Demon Island', a thinly veiled analogue of Pearl Harbor, which the Imperial Japanese Navy had attacked in December 1941. The horned 'Demons' are represented, satirically, as American sailors, one of whom bears a striking resemblance to the character of Bluto from the Fleischer Brothers' *Popeye* (1933–57) series.

Explicit children's propaganda films were made at other points by the Soviet Union and its satellites and in PRC China. Many such productions are concerned with the moment of communist revolution or with the proletarian struggle for it. A high proportion of PRC-era Chinese children's films are dramas of war and rebellion against the socio-economic status quo.

Typically, they centre on young protagonists fighting for a future communist utopia, often against brutal Japanese oppressors. In *Chicken Feather Letter* (*Jī máo xìn*, Shi Hui, 1954), a 12-year-old boy is entrusted with a message to deliver to the communist army in its battle against the Imperial Japanese Army. Although he is captured by the Japanese, he eventually escapes and leads them into a trap, and is able to deliver his message, which leads to the capture of an important Japanese military officer. In *Sparkling Red Star* (*Shǎnshǎn de hóngxīng*, Li Jun and Li Ang, 1974), a teenage boy, inspired by a red star given to him by his absent father as a symbol of the communist cause, rises up against a tyrannical landowner who has ransacked his village and murdered his mother (who is burned to death before his eyes). Marshalling a group of similarly downtrodden peasants as a guerrilla army, the boy succeeds in liberating several oppressed villages and in killing their persecutor, before finally joining his father in the Red Army to fight in the war against Japan. As Ting He explains, schools helped to distribute such films, organising free screenings to students: 'The viewings would take place during normal school hours so all the pupils were expected to attend. After the viewing, they were often required to submit their "reflections" – an essay to describe what they had learned from the film' (2013: 69). In these instances, film served as part of a structured programme of ideological learning alongside more traditional classroom activities.

Another tendency in communist propaganda film centres on inspirational pre-revolutionary figures. The DEFA film, *Moor and the Ravens of London* (*Mohr und die Raben von London*, Helmut Dziuba, 1968), is a hagiographic biopic of Karl Marx in his youth in London. In the film, Marx (known as 'Moor' because of his swarthy appearance) makes friends with a group of children working long hours, in appalling conditions, at a cotton mill. He also encounters a gang of juvenile thieves, the Ravens, whose theft of lace cloth from the mill is attributed to the young workers. Marx eventually persuades the Ravens to abandon their life of crime and to return to work; in the process, he exonerates the falsely accused children at the mill. Moreover, he enlists the help of a local government inspector to force the mill to cease its mistreatment of its workers. The film thus emphasises the importance of children becoming hard-working, law-abiding citizens, and reasserts the need to work together in a common cause. Equally, it presents a cursory warning on the intrinsic failures of capitalism. Greed, and the endless pursuit of profit, are seen to foment proletarian rebellion and,

The child as patriotic
citizen in *Sparkling
Red Star* (1974)

ultimately, reduce productivity. This version of Karl Marx is far from being a communist, but the events of the film suggest how revolutionary socialism might be seen as a logical, and even necessary, evolution in his worldview. Tellingly, perhaps, Socialist Party officials strongly disapproved of the film, believing that Marx was not portrayed in the heroic manner befitting his status as one of the architects of modern socialism. Consequently, the film was not shown in Moscow theatres to avoid the risk of alienating Soviet audiences, for whom this more humanistic portrayal of Marx was thought to be anathema (Blessing 2015: 160).

Of course, a high proportion of state-backed children's films support national ideologies in less explicit ways. The celebrated 1940s Soviet adaptation of *Cinderella* (*Zolushka*, Nadezhda Kosheverova and Mikhail Shapiro, 1947) is a notable example. Like many Soviet fairy tale films, the tone is comedic, often parodic. The film employs various forms of Brechtian distantiation: the artificiality of the sets, the intermixing of live-action and animation, the crude use of miniatures and rear projection, and the self-consciousness in performance (e.g. casting the 38-year-old actress, Yakima Zhejmo, as Cinderella). This self-consciousness is also present in the endearingly childlike tsar's closing, direct-to-camera monologue, which ironically draws attention to usually unspoken structural conventions – those of narrative closure and the provision of a moral lesson:

So, my dear friends, we've managed to get to the happy ending! Everybody's happy – except for the old hag, the forester's wife! But

The paternalistic young Karl Marx in *Moor and the Ravens of London* (1969)

it's her own fault – you know, connections are fine, but you have to have a conscience. When you'll be asked what you can actually do, what can you show? No connections will make your feet smaller, or your heart bigger or faithful. And the boy page will find happiness. The prince will have a daughter who looks like Cinderella, and the boy will fall in love with her when the time is right – and I'll be glad to marry him to my granddaughter, because I adore his beautiful soul and his faithful heart, integrity and affection. I adore these magical feelings which will never, never end!

This closing monologue seems broadly in accordance with Soviet ideals. However, there are ambiguities elsewhere in the narrative. As Prokhorov argues, by contrasting the childlike innocence of Cinderella and the tsar with the corruption of worldlier adult characters, such as the Stepmother, *Cinderella* restores 'the distinction between a child's and a grown-up's perspective at the world that Stalinist cinema for children tried so hard to efface' (2008: 140). Furthermore, although the benign foolishness of the tsar is not wholly incongruous with the tendency in Soviet fairy tale films, such as *The Humpbacked Horse* (*Konyok Gorbunok*, Ivan Ivanov-Vano, 1947), to portray rulers as incompetent, the character is unusual in two regards. Firstly, he is entirely sympathetic, and treats Cinderella's father, a woodcutter, as a friend and equal. Secondly, he remains tsar at the end of the film rather than being overthrown, as is more typical of the Soviet fairy tale.

The themes of war and revolution, and the strong connection between child and state ideology, that prevail in the Soviet and Chinese children's cinemas are almost wholly absent in the British and Indian traditions. The British CFF and the Indian CFSI, both of which began producing films during the 1950s, were afforded a high degree of creative autonomy, and their films are largely free from explicit politicking. Initially, most of their films were formally and ideological conventional, comprising simple adventure stories, primarily in a realist mode, where children learned important moral lessons within a clearly-established social framework in which structures of family and community were foregrounded. Both organisations favoured relatively simple film syntax, reflecting children's believed inability to process complex storylines, *mise-en-scène*, cinematography or editing patterns.

The CSFI's conservative approach was summed up in the 1970s by Kamini Kaushal, the former chair of the organisation:

> A good children's film should have an easy narrative style, a fair proportion of close-ups, a somewhat slow pace, preferably no flashbacks, an element of anticipation, abundant action and excitement, few dialogues, a good deal of humour and straight-forward and bright photography, preferably in colour. (Mulay 1981)

These principles are reflected the relative generic standardisation of its films. The Society's first production, *Jaldeep* (Kedar Sharma, 1956) – which won the Best Children's Film award at the 1957 Venice International Film Festival – is a straightforward morality play in which an arrogant, reckless youth learns necessary virtues of temperance and responsibility from an older male figure. A high proportion of CFSI features are small-scale dramas centring on pre-adolescent children and their interactions with the adult world, often set in small, self-contained rural or impoverished communities. Some CFSI films, it should be acknowledged, break this mould. The Hindi-language 1970s film, *Charandas Chor* (Shyam Benegal, 1975), is an allegorical fantasy derived from classical Indian folk tale. Generally, however, the Society has eschewed the non-realist conventions of the so-called 'Masala' style – with its emphases on song-and-dance – that predominates in commercial Indian cinema. CFSI films often develop a close relationship between child and a benevolent adult who serves as a figure of education and moral authority. The Malayalam-language CFSI production, *Keshu* (Sivan, 2009), centres on a mischievous, profoundly deaf and mute boy whose family views him as lazy and unintelligent. It is incumbent upon an enlightened outsider, an art teacher, to re-educate the boy's parents regarding his individual learning needs, and to imbue the child with sufficient confidence to allow his natural talent as an artist to shine through. The film thus allegorises the socialisation process (the child's graduation from childish misadventure, and his growing awareness of his responsibilities and vocation as a future adult citizen) while emphasising the need for adults to treat children with compassion and understanding.

Like the CSFI, the CFF was guided by a liberal humanistic worldview that upheld children's individualism while seeking to cultivate good moral and civic values in its audiences ('intimacy with good example', as the organisation's motto had it). During the 1950s, CFF films were predominantly middlebrow, emphasising middle-class values of taste and decency. Representations of adventurous, but unfailingly polite, children, affirmations of benign authority (especially policemen), strongly maintained boundaries between good and evil, and a prevailing realist aesthetic – in which fantastic or fairy tale tropes were determinedly excluded – were prominent characteristics. According to Mary Field, the CFF's first chief executive, 'To achieve that sense of security for which they crave, young children like to think of a world divided into the good, who in the long run win, and the bad, who eventually lose' (1952: 87). Unlike J. Arthur Rank, Field did not view her remit as explicitly educational, but there was always a strongly didactic underpinning. Indeed, at times CFF films reinscribe the social inequalities the organisation claimed to repudiate. Throughout the 1950s, there were very few working-class or non-white performers in sympathetic roles. Many of the films' villains were crude caricatures, such as the black tribal leader in *On the Run* (Pat Jackson, 1968). In these instances, 'Otherness' – deviations from the white, middle-class norm – serves as convenient shorthand for 'badness'.

During the 1960s and 1970s, the organisation extended its narrative and generic horizons, branching out into new genres, such as sports films, science-fiction and fantasy. It also introduced a more inclusive casting policy, hiring children with regional accents and from different ethnic backgrounds. Equally, the explicit didacticism of the earlier films was replaced, progressively, by an ethos of entertainment rather than of instruction.

High-spirited, action-oriented fantasy films like *Sammy's Super T-Shirt* (Jeremy Summers, 1978) and *A Hitch in Time* (Jan Darnley-Smith, 1978) were not markedly different in tone to contemporaneous Disney films such as *The Cat from Outer Space* (Norman Tokar, 1978) and *Unidentified Flying Oddball* (Russ Mayberry, 1979). These changes did not merely bespeak a shift in the culture within the organisation, or even the influence of Hollywood blockbuster family films such as *Star Wars*, which succeeded in addressing a mainstream market that the CFF – with its coterie audience of children's matinee attendees – was unable to capture. It also reflected a growing conviction, common to neo-liberal economies internationally, that the state has no business disseminating its governing ideology through propaganda films (not in peacetime, at least).

During the 1970s, the distinctions between state-funded and commercial children's cinema became less pronounced. In Britain, for instance, many of the post-1960 films distributed by the CFF were produced by independent producers (e.g. Michael Powell, Pat Jackson) who spent most of their career working in commercial cinema. Films that were more 'commercial' in style, if not in provenance, were released with greater regularity, such as the state-supported cycle of sci-fi and fantasy productions made in Britain, China and Soviet Russia during the 1980s. In countries such as India, Denmark and China, state-backed children's cinema still has an instrumental role in helping into production projects that would not receive funding in the commercial marketplace. There are still, of course, clear points of difference. State-funded films are usually made with fewer resources (e.g. smaller budget; the lack of experienced or top-line creative and technical personnel) and are predicated to a much greater degree on representations of children and their experiences.

But the broad shift from didacticism to escapism during the latter part of the twentieth century also reflects the influence of commercial children's films – or, more particularly, the dominance of the Hollywood family film. With their high production values, international casts and transnational appeal, Hollywood films have had a major impact on state-supported children's cinema. Firstly, in aesthetic terms they have made virtually everything else look like a poor relation. Secondly, their ubiquity has eroded the political will for state involvement, since they fulfil several – though certainly not all – of the instrumental functions of children's cinema. In the twenty-first century, even where state-supported children's cinema endures in some form (as in China, India and much of Scandinavia), it co-exists with, and is largely overshadowed by, commercial enterprise. The implications of this trend will be explored in the final chapter.

Nation, Culture and Commerce: Three Films

How, then, were questions of nation and identity negotiated in twentieth-century commercial children's cinema? This section presents case studies of three iconic non-Hollywood films: the German production, *Emil and the Detectives* (*Emil und die Detektive*, Gerhard Lamprecht, 1931); the French production, *The Red Balloon* (*Le Ballon Rouge*, Albert Lamorisse, 1956); and the Indian production, *The Adventures of Goopy and Bagha* (*Goopy Gyne Bagha Byne*, Satyajit Ray, 1969). Each represents a different facet of the relationship between commercial production and nation and culture. They were made in different nations, in different languages, and in different historical periods. Unlike the films discussed above, they were produced independently of the state and for commercial exhibition, rather than for specialised children's programmes; therefore, they were accessible to audiences of all types. Furthermore, they were manufactured in mixed economies with access to international distribution avenues closed to countries such as Soviet Russia, Czechoslovakia, East Germany and China; this is an important point when considering their global popularity. The three films are highly distinct from one another in terms of style and story. Each draws on different generic traditions: *Emil and the Detectives* on sentimental realism, *The Red Balloon* on symbolic fantasy, and *The Adventures of Goopy and Bagha* on allegorical fairy tale. However, they share various aspects that locate them within the broader structuring conventions of the children's film.

In their international popularity, these films might be seen as precursors to the contemporary productions discussed in the final chapter. However, they are distinct in two key regards. Firstly, their international recognition was highly atypical for children's films not distributed by Hollywood studios. Secondly, and most crucially, this recognition was largely contained to adult centres of discourse such as reviews, festival awards, educators and matinee programmers, and was mostly qualitative rather than economic. Indeed, they have more in common with the films discussed elsewhere in this chapter than with transnational, family-oriented franchises such as

Star Wars and *Harry Potter*. They are low-budget, made by small studios or by independent producers and are explicitly child-oriented.

They also advance different conceptions of childhood. *Emil and the Detectives* weighs the basic goodness and innate decency of its pre-adolescent protagonist, Emil (Rolf Wenkhaus), against his innate predilection for mischief and misadventure. It places emphasis on learned (socialised) behaviours: the boy adores his mother, and places his unwavering faith in responsible adults, such as the police – representatives of the state – as arbiters of justice and benign authority. However, the film divagates from most state-produced children's films in situating its protagonist partially outside the bounds of adult society. Most of the time, he has to rely either on his own resources or on those of other children. As such, it nostalgically evokes memories of childhood in adults – as Twain intended with *Tom Sawyer* – while celebrating the agency and competence of children, particularly when working together in a common cause. Equally, *Emil and the Detectives* is concerned with evoking the *realities* of childhood, moving beyond the largely allegorical or symbolic representations of children more characteristic of the socialist propaganda film. Long passages are given over to nostalgic explorations of the minutia of childhood: the excitement of embarking on long train journeys to the big city, the paternalistic indulgence of older family members, and the milieu of children's gangs with their internal politics, elaborate schemes, code words, disguises and so on.

In contrast, *The Red Balloon* views childhood, more symbolically, as a potential site of alienation, segregation and victimhood. The close affiliation between children and the upstanding representatives of adulthood in *Emil and the Detectives* is largely absent here. Children have the capacity for cruelty and destructiveness as well as for kindness and understanding. Of course, representations of corrupted childhood derive force from their incongruity with the Romantic (Blake, Wordsworth) archetype, which idyllically construes childhood as conterminous with goodness, innocence and unfettered play. Finally, *The Adventures of Goopy and Bagha* is rooted in another dominantly recurring archetype of childhood: as a symbolic period – here represented by childlike grown-ups – in which pre-social, natural desires are given free rein outside the bounds of mainstream society. In this tradition, there is always the potential for anarchism. To this extent, it is distantly related to Twain's construction of childhood misadventure in *The Adventures of Huckleberry Finn* (1884), and more closely affiliated with comic depictions of adults as symbolic children in, say, the Hollywood Three Stooges films (1930–65) or the Brazilian Trapalhões (1966–99) series.

These three films are worth examining in turn. *Emil and the Detectives*, adapted from Erich Kästner's 1929 novel by Billy Wilder and Emeric Pressburger (later major figures in the Hollywood and British cinemas, respectively), centres on a pre-adolescent boy, Emil Tischbein, who is sent by his mother (Käthe Haack) from their home in the provincial town of Neustadt to stay with his grandmother in Berlin during the school holidays. Travelling alone on the train, Emil is given drugged sweets by the sinister Mitlinski (Fritz Rasp), who then steals some money entrusted to him by his mother. When Emil regains consciousness, the train has arrived in Berlin, and Mitlinski has gone. Giving chase, Emil encounters a band of local children, the Detectives, who agree to help him recover his money. In the novel's most iconic moment, faithfully recreated, an increasingly anxious Mitlinski, on his way to the bank to deposit the money, finds himself pursued through the city streets by hordes of children. A chase, which begins slowly and quietly, builds to a frenzied extreme as both parties quicken their pace. Mitlinski takes refuge at the bank, but Emil proves to the clerk that the stolen money is his. The criminal flees, but is restrained by the huge gang of children waiting outside, and is led away by the police. It transpires that Mitlinski is a fugitive bank robber, with a 1000 marks reward on his head. In the film's final scene, Emil and his friends are fêted at a civic ceremony held in their honour in Emil's home town.

The film was warmly received both nationally and internationally. One German critic wrote:

Whoever has seen Lamprecht's work with those children can appreciate how much sacrificial love and patience he put into this celluloid. He has not tried to make stars or actors out of children, has not led them to mime in close-ups: rather they should be completely natural, and that they are. (Willig 2013)

Similarly, the British newspaper, *The Observer*, felt that it was 'the complete child's picture', and the *New York Times* called it 'delightful' and praised the technical quality (Lejeune 1933; Hall 1931). Gillian Lather has argued that the cross-cultural, cross-generational appeal of the story lies in its 'underlying faith in childhood that the otherwise cynical Kästner maintained throughout his life' (2004: 116).

It is central to the film's naturalistic evocation of childhood that it understands children's capacity, and desire, for degrees of disobedience. The film begins with a scene of authority subverted: Emil and his friends torment a pompous police officer by defacing a statue, dressing it in a flat cap and a Kaiser Wilhelm-like moustache. Emil's devotion to his mother is not in question, but his typicality as a boy on the cusp of adolescence is illustrated by his returning home late only just in time to catch the bus to Berlin, remarking that the person who invented uncomfortable Sunday suits ought 'to be killed', and impishly addressing his mother as 'Frau Tischbein'. Emil and the gang are intermediaries between two extreme but enduring child archetypes. The first is the sweetly 'innocent' Enlightenment-influenced figure of Victorian- and Edwardian-era children's literature; the second is epitomised by Huck Finn, who lives partially outside the social system and beyond the confines of institutions such as family, church and school.

The Detectives share some of Huck Finn's self-reliance, but (like Tom Sawyer) they remain strongly embedded within the social institutions Huck rejects as conformist and constraining. In one exchange, Emil explains his relationship with his mother to another boy, the Professor:

Emil: If only we'd found the money. I don't want my mother to...
Professor: Afraid of her, huh?
Emil: Me, afraid of my mother? No. She's constantly working, but we still don't have enough to get by. Losing those 140 marks is the same as you losing a million or even more.
Professor: You and your mother seem to be very close.
Emil: Colossally. But that doesn't make me a mummy's boy – whoever doubts that will be thrown against the wall!

The macho desire for self-reliance, and the boys' natural rejection of effeminising sentimentality, is counterbalanced by the intergenerational affinity between child and parent. The Detectives' parents are clearly well aware of the elaborate games in which their children are partaking. In one revealing sequence, when the mother and father of one of the Detectives (who has been manning a phone at 'home base') finds him asleep at his desk, drowsily repeating the code word 'Emil', indulgently they put him to bed. Such games, it is realised, are part of the formative years of any citizen.

While *Emil and the Detectives* is primarily oriented to *boyhood* misadventure, Emil's cousin, Pony Hütchen (Inge Landgut), emerges as an important character in the second half of the film. It is she, not their grandmother, who has the initiative to track down Emil; who possesses the moral authority to scold him for his recklessness; and, in a prefiguring of her presumed maternal duties, who brings food for the Detectives while they stake out Mitlinski's hotel. However, her agency is matched by awareness of the social restrictions preventing girls from engaging in such activities. After feeding the gang, she announces: 'A good girl belongs in bed; if two kids went missing in one day, it would be a bit much for grandma.' She is, however, allowed a mildly picaresque moment in the film's closing scene, where she intervenes in a fight for her affections between Emil and Gustav with the words, 'As long as you're still rascals, I'll take you both!'

These boys may be rascals, but the film's implicit didacticism is located in their capture of Mitlinksi. Collectively, they outmanoeuvre a contemptible malefactor, and this action underlines their capacity for justice, determination and agency. This is a victory of the underdog that addresses adults' nostalgia for their own childhood, and speaks to children's own desire for power and agency. But it can also be interpreted, in a wider sense, as asserting the essential goodness of the next generation. These children will inherit a damaged, war-torn nation (and Kästner could not have predicted the coming of World War II) but appear up to the task of rebuilding it with necessary virtues of hard work, planning and unity of purpose. This scene at the police station, in which the boys are congratulated for their enterprise in catching Mitlinski, and are praised as being 'Just like real detectives', celebrates their civic mindedness, and their impending future as good citizens. But through their common goals, allied to their natural attributes, the children succeed where the adult establishment fails.

Like *Emil and the Detectives*, *The Red Balloon* is one of the very few non-Hollywood children's films to attain lasting international recognition. Upon initial release, it won the Palme d'Or for best short film, the Oscar for Best Original Screenplay (the only time the award has been won by a short) and numerous critics' awards worldwide. It has also been adapted for the British stage by the National Theatre, remade as a French-Taiwanese film

The companionable relationship at the centre of *The Red Balloon* (1956)

(*Flight of the Red Balloon*, Hou Hsiao-Hsien, 2007), shown widely on TV globally and become a perennial subject for exhibition in children's matinees. The film centres on the friendship between a young Parisian boy and a large, perfectly spherical, red balloon he discovers tied to a lamppost. As with most silent-era films, *The Red Balloon* tells its story primarily through visual means. Dialogue is kept to a minimum, and the narrative is simple and easily grasped. It deals with psychological realities explicable to audiences of almost any age or background: the desire for deep and intimate friendship; the fear of loneliness and alienation; a yearning for transcendence from the mundane and the everyday, and for the possibility of magic and adventure.

However, despite its apparent universalism, it is not quite accurate to speak of the film as being stateless or ahistorical. The Parisian setting is unmistakeable, as is its post-war milieu. Filmed in the slightly dilapidated neighbourhood of Ménilmontant in washed-out, wintery greys (dominated by concrete and threateningly cloudy skies), the film juxtaposes the after-effects of World War II – its resonances of social alienation, economic depression and urban decay – with the possibility, and the hope, of recovery. This spirit of optimism is localised in the figure of the boy protagonist, Pascal (played by, and named after, Lamorisse's own son), and the vividly red, anthropomorphised balloon. The human impulse towards callousness and destruction, conversely, is embodied in the gang of schoolchildren who mercilessly pursue the balloon, and eventually succeed in destroying it. In the final scene, the film moves into redemptive fantasy, with balloons of all colours gathering to take the boy on a magical flight over the metropolis.

Essentially, *The Red Balloon* is an analogue of the animal film, a prevalent sub-genre of the children's movie. In such films, the companion (here balloon; elsewhere animal) is a psychological mirror of the child protagonist. In *The Red Balloon*, this companionable relationship compensates for the lack of friendship elsewhere in Pascal's life. Most of the adults in the film are remote: his mother, who insists that the balloon is kept out of the apartment (the animal metaphor is at its clearest here); the schoolteacher, who will not allow it to remain outside the school entrance; and the churchman who ejects both Pascal and the balloon from the cathedral. The vivid redness of the balloon contrasts with the film's overriding greyness, and mirrors the child's extraordinariness in a world that, at best, evokes dull conformity, and at its worst malicious destruction.

The Red Balloon has much in common with child-centred but adult-oriented films such as *The 400 Blows* (*Les Quatre Cents Coups*, François Truffaut, 1959), *Kes* (Ken Loach, 1969) and *Pixote* (Héctor Babenco, 1981). In each case, the alienation of the child protagonist operates as a metaphor for wider social malfunction. Pascal is intelligent, receptive and imaginative; his isolation marks him out as a non-conformist. The lack of empathy or kindness among the adults, and the unblunted destructiveness of the children, emphasises the relationship between Pascal and the balloon. Like the boy, the balloon is isolated, curious and vulnerable. To this extent, both present a sharp contrast with the gang of children that mercilessly pursues the balloon. In *Emil and the Detectives*, the potentiality of children as social collective is celebrated. Here, collective action is equated with conformity and violence – a reaction, perhaps, to the vision of millions of youth marching in tune to nationalist ideology during World War II. *The Red Balloon*'s final scene might be taken as a literal 'rising above', a metaphorical act of separation which divorces the child from the greyness, alienation and destruction represented by the post-war city. The multitude of differently-coloured balloons joining together in Pascal's cause might also serve as a metaphor for racial egalitarianism, in which case the film's plangent appeal for the future utopia acquires additional layers of meaning.

If *The Red Balloon* approaches universality, *The Adventures of Goopy and Bagha* is highly localised in its modes of appeal. Directed by the great Bengali filmmaker, Satyajit Ray, the film is a loose adaptation of a story written in 1915 by Ray's grandfather, the writer and painter Upendrokishore Ray. Trading particularly on Bengali folkloric tradition (music, wordplay, costume and dance), the film centres on two down-at-heel peasants, Goopy (Tapan Chatterjee) and Bagha (Robi Ghosh), both of whom have high musical ambition but no talent, and who are exiled from their communities for making a nuisance of themselves. While sleeping in a forest, they are visited by the supernatural King of Ghosts, who grants them three special powers: the ability to transport themselves anywhere in the world, to make food and drink magically appear by clapping their hands, and to entrance any listener with their music. Having fed and clothed themselves, Goopy and Bagha use their musical talents to prevent a war between two kingdoms, and, in the film's final scene, both marry beautiful princesses.

Produced in black and white on a very low budget, the film is one of Ray's lesser-known productions in the West. However, it is vastly popular in Bengal, where it had the longest run ever for a Bengali film upon initial release, prompting Ray to remark that: 'It is extraordinary how quickly it has become part of popular culture. Really there isn't a single child in the city who doesn't know and sing the songs' (Robinson 1989: 182–83). More recently, the story's English translator, Swagata Deb, recalled that: 'As children we loved the film. The characters were adorable, the music was out of this world and the dance that the ghosts danced was a delightful play of light and shadow and was something that we had never seen before' (Roychoudhuri 2015). However, the film was unable to find a distributor in Britain or the United States, where Ray's stock as an 'auteur' was at its highest. When it was finally screened at part of the London Film Festival in 1980, Ray estimated that 90 per cent of the audience were Bengalis

(Robinson 1989: 182–83). This indifference is probably attributable, to some degree, to a familiar, elitist disregard for children's fiction, for the narrative adopts a familiar fairy tale structure: a rags-to-riches story of simple, virtuous protagonists (symbolic, not literal, children), in which evil is defeated – albeit, unusually, through peaceful means rather than by violent action – and a happy ending is supplied.

However, the film's relatively lowly status also reflects its cultural specificities. The centrepiece is the six-minute 'Dance of the Ghosts' scene, which Ray himself went as far as to describe as 'surely the most striking thing ever done in cinematic choreography' (Robinson 1989: 186). In this abstract, surrealist montage sequence, spirits of the forest, in traditional Bengali attire and ghostly make-up, perform a series of traditional dances against expressionistic backdrops. The effects are rudimentary; Ray shoots much of the sequence in negative in order to imbue it with the desired sense of dislocation, and distorts the image in various other ways. But there are clear political undercurrents here. Ray presents four classes of ghosts, each obliquely representing one of the four *varnas* (classes) of Hinduist doctrine: *Brahmins* (priests, scholars and teachers); *Kshatriyas* (nobles or warriors); *Vaishyas* (commoners or merchants); and *Shudras* (labourers and service providers). The sequence ends with the representatives of each class hierarchically positioned from top to bottom in the frame, but Ray inverts the orthodoxy in positioning the workers at the top, and the rulers at the bottom. This scene prefigures the eventual triumph of the initially down-at-heel Goopy and Bagha over the despotic aristocrats of the enemy kingdom. It may also be taken as a coded affirmation of changing social structures, or perhaps even the anticipated disintegration of the Indian caste system.

The Adventures of Goopy and Bagha is rarely polemical. Its protagonists know little about politics, and their desires (for music, comfort, beauty, richness) are essentially childlike, and embrace a kind of utopian egalitarianism, symbolised by the unifying power of their music. In one of their songs, which they play to the Maharaja and with which they enchant the entire court, they sing:

It's the language of rhythm, the language of rhyme
The language of singing while the drum beats time
Young and old, rich and poor, take it to their heart.

Another of their songs contains the anti-materialist lyric:

What makes people sad?
Not only when things go wrong
But piles of money stored away can make you unhappy.

Yet, to some degree, the liberal politics of the film are subordinated to the governing conventions of the fairy tale source narrative. Social equality may implicitly be endorsed, but the ideological status quo is ultimately reaffirmed. Goopy and Bagha not only uphold the governing class structure (albeit a benign iteration of it) but are actually absorbed into it through their marriages to the princesses.

In this respect, the film bears interesting comparison with its sequel, *Kingdom of Diamonds* (*Hirak Rajar Deshe*, Ray, 1980), which is much more explicitly a socialist parable of political and economic oppression of the lower classes by the ruling elite. Its antagonist, the ruler of the eponymous kingdom of diamonds, has amassed obscene wealth at the expense of his subjects. The King has also closed down all the schools in the kingdom, and invented a machine to brainwash anyone who opposes him. Eventually, Goopy and Bagha manage to turn the King's machine against him, turning him into a benevolent ruler. What is ultimately presented here is a form of socio-economic levelling. The reformed King largely divorces himself from materialist concerns and redistributes his wealth amongst his people. Furthermore, the climactic scene in which he helps to pull down his own marble statue symbolises his voluntary diminution in power and status, and the explicit establishment of a socialist utopia. According to Ashish Rajadhyaksha, Ray's decision to return to Goopy and Bagha in the wake of Indira Gandhi's notorious, unilateral 'Emergency' of 1975–77 was widely viewed in India as 'withdrawal' from politics 'into the relatively uncontroversial area of commercially successful children's films' (1996: 682–84). But this is hardly a 'withdrawal'; rather, it represents a conscious decision to channel political comment through allegory. For the film's producers, the assumption that children's cinema must be devoid of serious meaning serves to protect them from accusations of articulating politically sensitive or seditious comment. Actor Uptal Dutta, who played the King, described the film as 'out-and-out political', and Ray admitted that, 'In a fantasy one can be forthright [...] but if you're dealing with contemporary

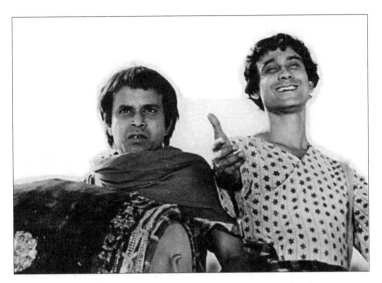

Satyajit Ray's symbolic children in *The Adventures of Goopy and Bagha* (1969)

characters, you can be articulate only up to a point because of censorship. You simply cannot attack the party in power' (Robinson 1989: 188).

Here, as in many of the state-sanctioned films discussed earlier in the chapter, children's film is a vehicle through which political doctrine may be expressed more forcefully than in mainstream popular cinema. In the children's propaganda film, child figures – real or symbolic – remain powerful symbolic presences. Children's support of the state apparatus in the Soviet and PRC China productions serves as ultimate proof of its legitimacy, since, by implication, children are guided only by their innate goodness and innocence, and are untainted by worldly corruption. In contrast, in films that articulate criticisms of society, such as *The Adventures of Goopy and Bagha* and *Kingdom of Diamonds*, childlike figures are able to penetrate through the layers of ideological mystification in ways that adult characters cannot. This recognition of the symbolic power of the child is shared by almost all children's films, regardless of language, nation or culture.

4 CONTEMPORARY CHILDREN'S CINEMA: NATIONAL AND TRANSNATIONAL TRENDS

Today, children's cinema is viewed primarily through a commercial lens. The social and educative imperatives that characterised twentieth-century production are now far less visible: Since the 1980s, most children's films internationally have been produced not under the auspices of the nation-state, but by an oligopoly of multimedia conglomerates concerned with profit rather than pedagogy. While non-commercial children's films are still made and continue to find limited distribution in schools and festivals, contemporary children's cinema is characterised by a different, though equally fundamental, duality – one that has partly superseded the old antithesis between commercial and non-commercial production. There is an enduring desire for children's films to reflect the values and customs of the culture and society in which they are produced and which, ostensibly, they serve. But there is a felt incompatibility between this familiar emphasis on films reflecting cultural heritage and the apparent economic necessity for them to transcend regional specificities (in style, idiom and ideology) and reach a larger, transnational market. The need to balance fiscal considerations while presenting an attractive, exportable image of local culture for global consumption is a perennial point of tension in concepts of 'national' cinema.

This chapter presents an overview of how national traditions of children's cinema have negotiated transnational trends. 'Transnationalism' is a nebulous concept; it may refer to the international nature of economic and industrial transaction, or to the less concrete practice of cultural exchange.

In both domains, the United States has been accused of 'imperialism'. At the time of writing, Hollywood blockbusters comprise 100 per cent of the top 30 films at the global box office. This figure is admittedly skewed by the fact that the North American box office still makes up almost 50 per cent of the global market for theatrically-released feature films. Nevertheless, most of Hollywood's biggest hits are family films, and this has tended to shift the terms of the debate to a perennially sensitive subject: the consumption habits of children in relation to mass-produced culture.

The market supremacy of Hollywood family films has long promoted anxiety regarding the survival prospects for independent children's films. Objections have also been levelled at the aggressively 'protectionist' policies of the major Hollywood studios. In 2003, Anna Home, chief executive of the Children's Film and Television Foundation (CFTF), condemned the practice of US studios optioning 'practically everything' from the stable of British children's fiction, adding that 'British children are missing out culturally by existing on a diet of US films' (Chrisafis 2003). The importance of a sustainable, indigenous children's cinema has also been highlighted by leading industry figures in Denmark (Vivarelli 2007), Brazil (Ortiz Ramos 2004: 132) and India ('Clean Films').

Transnationalism takes various forms. These include (but are not limited to) modes of production, distribution and exhibition; narration and narrative; international locations; international viewing practices; and transnational stars and directors. Deborah Shaw (2013) points out that films may also involve transregional exchange (e.g. the distribution of Bollywood films across Asia), or be founded on transnational collaboration. She also notes that films may indeed still be 'national', rather than 'transnational', if they are produced through national finance initiatives for local or regional distribution, made in a national idiom or focus on issues of national interest. Indeed, whilst Hollywood has often publicly asserted its universalism, and some Japanese commentators have referred to anime as '*mukokuseki*' ('stateless'), cinema must always embody, however obliquely, aspects of the national character (Napier 2005: 22).

Nevertheless, the national/transnational dialectic remains a useful prism through which to view developments in contemporary children's film. We might identify four standard positions assumed by national cinemas in relation to Hollywood: i) differentiation, in which films are thematically or aesthetically distinct; ii) competition, which encompasses non-Hollywood films produced with the populist aesthetic and narrative transparency that characterises mainstream Hollywood cinema, and/or are promoted aggressively; iii) co-operation, which includes distribution deals between Hollywood studios and non-Hollywood production companies; and iv) assimilation, which involves the acquisition, in whole or part, of non-Hollywood production companies by Hollywood firms. In some cases, though, this Hollywood-world antithesis is misleading. As we saw in Chapter 2, post-1980s multimedia conglomeration has decentralised film production. While Hollywood remains the nominal centre of the US film industry, a large percentage of its films are produced in other countries, making use of specialist technical facilities (e.g. Leavesden Studios in England or WETA Digital in New Zealand) and cheaper sources of labour (e.g. in Prague). Furthermore, with the exception of Disney, none of the parent companies of the 'big six' major studios are based in Hollywood (Sony's headquarters are in Tokyo).

Conglomerates such as Disney now favour a multilayered production policy. While continuing to produce recognisably 'Hollywood' films made in the 'classical' style, they also invest heavily in family-oriented films produced by *non-Hollywood* studios felt to possess international box office appeal. Examples include Disney's distribution deal with the renowned Japanese anime production company, Studio Ghibli; Warner Bros.' investment and distribution deal with Heyday Films, the British company that produced the *Harry Potter* series; and British animation studio Aardman's funding and distribution deals with DreamWorks and Sony. A third approach is investment in 'national' films produced in the local idiom (language, style) by companies in which Hollywood studios hold a financial stake or a controlling interest. In 2011, Disney acquired the Indian media company, UTV, and promptly announced a programme of Indian films 'that embody Disney brand values – optimistic, fun, meaningful and emotional entertainment for the entire family' ('Walt Disney, UTV'). Similarly, in 2012, DreamWorks entered the Chinese animation industry by co-founding Oriental DreamWorks with a consortium of Chinese investment companies. Oriental DreamWorks's first production, *Kung Fu Panda 3* (Jennifer Yuh Nelson and Alessandro Carloni, 2016), became the highest-grossing animated film in China, underlining the potential profitability of this strategy.

Children's films and family films remain at the forefront of developments both in 'national' and 'transnational' cinemas. Small-scale, state-funded children's films are often construed as the quintessence of local or national cultural tradition. In contrast, big-budget family films represent a boundary-breaking universalism, cutting across divisions in age, sex, class, race and language. The continuation of state funding of children's films in India, China and Denmark – even at the low level at which it operates – represents not just an enduring belief in film's potentiality as a socialising apparatus, but also a conscious repudiation of cultural globalisation, crudely reified in the vision of Hollywood hegemony. It is this feared loss of local tradition that led, in 1993, to France announcing its 'cultural exception' (which held that cultural products should be exempt from free-trade agreements), and to China's ongoing import quota on foreign films.

Transnational Developments in Europe

With relatively free movement of capital and creative talent, European cinema has always been somewhat 'transnational' in character. Post-1980s policies of financial deregulation have left British studios reliant on cutting international co-production and distribution deals. Elsewhere in Europe, such enterprise has typically been accompanied by protectionist initiatives promoting a pan-European cinema based on a mixed economic model of centralised organisation and funding boosted by private finance. The Council of Europe's Eurimages (1989–), and the European Union's MEDIA program (1990–), are designed to stimulate the European film market through assistance with funding and distribution.

One notable European attempt to rival Hollywood in the production of mainstream family films was the French-German-Italian film, *Asterix & Obelix vs. Caesar* (*Astérix & Obélix contre César*, Claude Zidi, 1999). Adapted from the best-selling comic books by René Goscinny and Albert Uzerdo, the $45 million film was the most expensive French-language film ever produced. That it was made with production and funding involvement from several companies across three European nations underpins the economic necessity of co-production. Indeed, *Asterix & Obelix vs. Caesar* received over €600,000 in financial assistance from Eurimages – a relatively insignificant proportion of the overall budget, but revealing in terms of its perceived cultural and commercial importance. The film eventually grossed over $100 million worldwide, with almost ten million theatrical admissions in France (where *Le Monde* identified it as 'the image of resistance to American cinematographic imperialism') (Riding 1999).

The film's popularity led to three sequels (2002–12) being produced, all of them highly successful in Europe but virtually unheard of in North America. The franchise's uneven income distribution says much about the US theatrical market's high barriers to entry, and North America's long-held disdain towards foreign language films. Nevertheless, the *Asterix* films appropriate several narrative and aesthetic strategies associated with Hollywood cinema, foregrounding spectacle (including CGI effects), international stars (e.g. Christian Clavier and Gérard Depardieu), broad comedy, and a 'high-concept' action/adventure fantasy premise. Its sequel, *Asterix & Obelix: Mission Cleopatra* (*Astérix & Obélix: Mission Cléopâtre*, Alain Chabat, 2002), retains these qualities but widens the appeal to teenage and adult audiences. The humour is more allusive, with a preponderance of intertextual references, in the style of recent Hollywood family films such as *Shrek* (Andrew Adamson and Vicky Jenson, 2001). Although some of the jokes are topical – e.g. references to France's 35-hour working week and industrial action – few are intelligible *only* to Francophone audiences. Indeed, the film's soundtrack is assuredly transnational, including familiar songs and musical motifs such as James Brown's 'I Got You (I Feel Good)', John Williams' 'Darth Vader' theme from *Star Wars*, and Boots Randolph's 'Yakety Sax' (a.k.a. 'the Benny Hill theme').

The English-language French animation, *Arthur and the Invisibles* (*Arthur et les Minimoys*, Luc Besson, 2006), is even more obviously pitched at the global market. Produced in English, the international *lingua franca*, it features international stars such the British child actor Freddie Highmore, Robert De Niro, Madonna and David Bowie. Unlike *Asterix*, it also received US distribution, yet it still vastly underperformed, with US grosses of just over $15 million. Most damagingly, the film failed to compete in Europe, with total European theatrical admissions in the region of eight million, compared with over 40 million for *Shrek 2* (Andrew Adamson, 2004) and *Ice Age: The Meltdown* (Carlos Saldanha, 2006) (Schöffel 2008). Yet *Arthur and the Invisibles* was still the second most-watched European children's or family film in Europe between 2004 and 2007, behind *Wallace & Gromit: The Curse of the Were-Rabbit* (Nick Park and Steve Box, 2005). Surveys commissioned by the European Children's Film Association (ECFA) reveal the extent to which European children's films struggle even to secure regional distribution. Of 90 European children's films produced in 2000–04, almost half were shown in only one other European country (Vanginderhuysen 2005). Similarly, of 161 films released in 2004–07, only 15 were screened in more than 10 countries in Europe, and less than half of these were distributed by independent companies. Overall, around 80 per cent of admissions for European children's films occur in the domestic market (ibid.). These figures would suggest that the pious hope of a pan-European network of film production and distribution has largely gone unrealised.

Britain, more than any other country outside the United States, has embraced a transnational aesthetic. 'Britishness', or more commonly 'Englishness', is central to the international appeal of the *Harry Potter* series and Aardman's Wallace and Gromit characters. Both support an attractive vision of heritage Britain that draws on recognisable landmarks and iconography; it is scarcely surprising that, as two of Britain's most lucrative cultural exports, they have been utilised in international tourism campaigns (O'Connor 2003; 'Wallace and Gromit'). Yet in both cases, the features are bankrolled by Hollywood: Warner Bros. in the case of the *Harry Potter* and *Fantastic Beasts* (2016–) series, and DreamWorks, and later Sony, with Aardman's animated features. The key question is the extent to which theme, narrative and ideology are dictated by commercial considerations. In the *Harry Potter* films, and in Aardman's Claymation feature, *The Curse of the Were-Rabbit*, national markers are largely associative or iconographic. Shots of Big Ben and London Bridge, the vaguely upper-class registers of Hogwarts and wizard society in *Harry Potter*, and the human protagonist's obsession with tea and cheese in *Wallace and Gromit*, bespeak a cosmetic 'Englishness' (as do costume, architecture and accents). These surface pleasures bear little connection with the everyday experiences of British people. Both *The Curse of the Were-Rabbit* and its precursor, *Chicken Run* (Nick Park and Peter Lord, 2000), ascribe to the storytelling conventions of Hollywood cinema, abandoning the narrative circularity of Aardman's Oscar-winning *Creature Features* (Nick Park, 1989) and *Wallace and Gromit* shorts in favour of goal-oriented protagonists, complicating action (based on conflict), narrative resolution and an emotive, 'feel-good' ending. *The Curse of the Were-Rabbit* also playfully alludes to internationally-known films such as *King Kong* (Merian C. Cooper and Ernest B. Schoedsack, 1933), *The Wolf Man* (George Waggner, 1941) and *The Fly* (David Cronenberg, 1986).

With its thematic focus on family and friendship, maturation, war, religion, extremism and concepts of good and evil, the *Harry Potter* series develops a socio-political-cultural pluralism. North America's cultural influence on modern Britain can be detected in many areas of narrative and production, such as the classically Hollywood action-adventure structure and trappings (e.g. costly CGI special effects). But these films invoke multi-cultural, multi-ethnic modes of representation. Much of the detail in the battle between Harry Potter and Lord Voldemort evokes the shock and awe of modern warfare and terrorism. The antithesis between Voldemort's 'pure-blood' movement and the 'mudbloods' contaminated by human inter-breeding might be seen to allegorise divisive racial tensions in countries and regions across the world, even if skin colour appears largely irrelevant in the fictional world of the films. And we cannot definitively state that the commodified Englishness of Hogwarts, or the inescapable iconographies of 9/11 associated with Lord Voldemort and his campaigns of terrorism, are *local* specificities. They are transnational currencies that transcend borders of culture and language.

The emergence of the Paris-based StudioCanal as a major player in European film production has reduced the prior dependence on Hollywood. By 2005, Canal+, which owns StudioCanal, was involved in financing 80 per cent of French films. In recent years, the company has moved purposely into the funding and distribution of big-budget family movies intended for the international market. Tellingly, several of its biggest hits have been produced in English, not French. *Paddington* (Paul King, 2014), adapted from British author Michael Bond's stories about a Peruvian bear living with an English family in London, was produced by Heyday Films (of *Harry Potter* fame), but distributed by StudioCanal. At the time of writing, it is the highest-grossing non-Hollywood family film ever released. Another StudioCanal film, Aardman's *Shaun the Sheep Movie* (Mark Burton and Richard Starzak, 2015), contains no dialogue whatsoever, thus sidestepping the need to produce costly foreign dubs, and allowing it to transcend linguistic borders.

These co-production initiatives remain the primary route in Europe to international recognition. However, a small minority of European children's films still come to prominence via positive word-of-mouth. The notoriously profane Danish animation, *Terkel in Trouble* (*Terkel i knibe*, Kresten Vestsbjerg Andersen et al., 2004), registered only around 450,000 admis-

The deliberately profane 'family film', *Terkel in Trouble* (2004)

sions (compared with almost 14 million for *The Curse of the Were-Rabbit*) on initial release, but became a cult hit after rave reviews. The success of such films often rests on their degree of incongruence from accepted standards of mainstream children's cinema and family entertainment. The film's British DVD release described it as 'The Psycho Family Film of the Year', deliberately emphasising its alterity in an arena often marked by bland conformity.

National Cinemas

Despite the distribution problems noted above, continental Europe remains the world centre for state-funded and independent children's cinema. Subsidies remain particularly high in Denmark and Sweden, where 25 per cent and 10 per cent of film subsidies, respectively, are allocated to children's and youth films. Most European cinemas have adopted a mixed economy model, integrating state funding with commercial partnerships. In Denmark, the two national broadcasters, DR and TV2, are frequent co-production partners, giving children's and youth films an outlet on television. Similarly, in Germany, films are often co-produced by television networks and are given special programming slots on Saturdays and on public holidays (Rössler et al. 2009: 36). The Berlin-based *Der besondere Kinderfilm* ('special children's film'), an association of public service broadcasters, funding organisations and representatives from the industry, also promotes the production of low-budget, independent films with original stories.

In Denmark, as in continental Europe more broadly, most children's films are small-scale and naturalistic, a fact perhaps jointly attributable to meagre resources and to the strong tradition of realism in European cinema. The box office failure of the animated feature, *Valhalla* (Peter Madsen and Jeffrey J. Varab, 1986), probably played a part in Denmark's strategic rejection of transnational modes of production. Co-directed by a former Disney animator, *Valhalla* was the costliest Danish film ever made, and whilst it was highly popular in its home market, it was barely seen outside of Scandinavia. Most Danish children's and youth films are closer in philosophy to another foundational production, *Rubber Tarzan* (*Gummi Tarzan*, Søren Kragh-Jacobsen, 1981), a story about a young boy who fails to match up to his father's idealised conception of masculinity and who is bullied at school for his weakness, but who eventually learns the lesson that 'Everybody's good as something – you just have to discover what it is'.

The metanarrative of the child coming to terms with his or her place in the world is prominent in such films, but there are two other notable trends in recent production. Firstly, as in Hollywood, standards of acceptability have liberalised, so that taboo themes that would once have been dealt with only abstractly (if at all) are now engaged with directly. This is partly a consequence of the realisation that children cannot entirely be 'protected' from harsh or discomforting realities, but it also reflects the sizable adult market for theatrically-released and made-for-television films. In Denmark in 2007, 11 children's and youth films attracted 59 per cent of all theatrical admissions, and in 2014, German children's films comprised 7 out of the top 20 films at the national box office (Rössler et al. 2009: 64; Kleber 2016). Whilst these economies of success are considerably less than for Hollywood family films, they do correspond with a broader, and undeniable, embrace of what is ostensibly children's culture among audiences of all ages. In Denmark, in particular, the boundaries between 'children's film' and 'adult film' are virtually non-existent. The Danish Film Institute's Flemming Kaspersen (2012) has suggested that 'good children's films are good grownup films too. This means that they don't talk down to the audience, they don't censor their own language or aesthetics and they don't compromise the story'. While such comments are made in relation to an unusually liberal system of film censorship, they nonetheless gesture to a possible future (however unlikely it may presently seem) in which the cultural barriers between childhood and adulthood break down altogether.

The second notable trend is that, whilst such films almost always end with a rapprochement between children and adults, child protagonists are afforded greater independence in ability and in moral authority. In the Danish film, *We Shall Overcome* (*Drømmen*, Niels Arden Oplev, 2006), a group of children inspired by Martin Luther King's Civil Rights campaign rebel against a tyrannical schoolmaster. Here, youth represents the possibility of a less bigoted or authoritarian future, echoing interwar and postwar European films such as *Emil and the Detectives*, *Hue and Cry* (Charles Crichton, 1947) and *The Red Balloon*. In the Swedish film, *Kidz in Da Hood* (*Förortsungar*, Catti Edfeldt and Ylva Gustavsson, 2006), a multiethnic gang of suburban children exhibit greater acceptance of racial and cultural 'otherness' than the authorities, which attempt to deport an orphaned ten-year-old girl from Sierra Leone. And in the German film, *Fiddlesticks* (*Quatsch und die Nasenbärbande*, Veit Helmer, 2014), a group of six pre-school children rebel against the plasticity of a modern consumer culture endorsed by their parents. Equally, in several recent films, children's relationship with their parents is closer to that of equals than subordinates. In the British *Nanny McPhee* (Kirk Jones, 2005) and the French-Canadian *The Pee-Wee 3D* (Éric Tessier, 2012), empathetic and emotionally mature children help to rehabilitate their grieving fathers after the death of their wives.

Whereas European children's cinema has survived recent economic uncertainties, the collapse of the Soviet Union and its mechanisms of state support led to a vacuum in Eastern European children's film that commercial enterprise has largely been unable to fill. As Gabriele Röthemeyer has observed, 'entire areas became blank spots', including the Czech and Slovak Republics, the Baltic countries, the Ukraine, Belarus and Kazakhstan (1996: 179–81). But since the turn of the millennium, commercial children's film in Russia has gradually reasserted itself. Having to compete with imported Hollywood fare, most contemporary Russian child-oriented films are levelled at cross-demographic audiences. But there is an important point of difference from the British and pan-European models: Russian family films are produced almost exclusively for the domestic market.

The child as 'other' in *Kidz in Da Hood* (2006)

The *Three Bogatyrs* film series (2004–), produced by the St. Petersburg-based Melnitsa Animation Studios, is a keynote of post-Soviet Russian cinema. The films are loosely adapted from Russian and Slavic folklore, particularly epic poetry. In aesthetic terms, they owe much to the rounded character animation of *Soiuzmul'tfilm* (which, in turn, was indebted to classical-era Disney). They are predominantly comic in tone, and heavily intertextual. The hero's line, 'I'll be back', in *Ilia Muromets i Solovei Razboinik* (Vladimir Toropchin, 2007), is an obvious parody of Arnold Schwarzenegger's line in *The Terminator* (James Cameron, 1984). Such referentiality playfully alludes to a transnational culture that the series appropriates and rejects in equal measure. The films' most popular characters in Russia are humourless, exaggeratedly masculine heroes, reflecting the broader national valorisation of the 'Iron Man'. Furthermore, they bespeak the strongly patriarchal tradition in Russian society, linking virtuous women – such as the wives of the three male heroes in *Tri Bogatyria i Shamakhanskaia Tsaritsa* (Sergei Glezin, 2010) – with domesticity. Finally, most of the series' antagonists are villainous, dark-skinned Turks, mirroring national fears concerning immigration. These films, as Natalie Kononenko concludes, are 'uniquely Russian' (2015: 184), representing a pseudo-revanchist riposte to the market-leading films imported from Hollywood.

Dark-skinned villainy in the Three Bogatyrs series

In India and China, children's films continue to receive a low level of state funding via the Children's Film Society, India (CFSI) and the China Film Group (CFG), which absorbed the China Children's Film Studio (CCFS) in 1998. State-funded productions in both companies have explored topics and themes overlooked by the commercial sector. Most CFSI films are still small-scale, slow-paced dramas centring on children and their experiences, and many CCFS films fall into the category of what Ting He calls 'good students at school' (2013: 120) films, focusing on the life of schoolchildren and their process of learning and maturation in school (a microcosm for society-at-large). But films like the CCFS's *The Atmospheric Layer Vanishes* (*Da qiceng xiaoshi*, Feng Xiaoning, 1990) are less conventional. Centering on the consequences of a major industrial accident that destroys the ozone layer, resulting in the imminent end of life on Earth, it is a rare instance of apocalyptic fiction in the children's film genre. The film bears comparison with the British Children's Film Foundation's production, *The Battle for Billy's Pond* (Harley Cokeliss, 1976), in its ecological themes, implicit assault on the amorality of advanced capitalism and industry, and its attempt to educate children on the necessities both of environmental awareness and non-violent protest. Director Feng Xiaoning intended the film as 'an alarm', a vehicle to 'show children what's what' (Donald 2005: 30). Such films demonstrate that cinema made in the service of the state has the capacity to be socially progressive, and not simply serve the vested interests of the dominant ideology.

In both countries, the commercialisation of film has decisively changed the relationship between cinema and spectator, with audiences (including children) viewed increasingly as autonomous consumers rather than as citizens of the state. During the early 1990s, trade barriers preventing the entry of Hollywood films were lowered. In China, this was partly a response to a recent recession in the film industry, after which the government permitted the importation of 10 foreign titles per year on a revenue-sharing basis (Ting He 2013: 10–11). The first wave of Hollywood films in China included *The Lion King* and *Toy Story*. In the first half of 1995, ticket sales rose by 50 per cent (Ting He 2013: 39). In India, a similar pattern emerges: *Jurassic Park* broke box office records for a foreign film, grossing over Rs. 50 million. The profitability of family films in these countries is only partly due to their narrative and aesthetic attractions. It also reflects more conservative attitudes towards violence and sexuality, which place limits on the distribution of adult-certificated films. More than half the Hollywood films imported by China in 2002–10 were family-oriented (ibid.).

Commercial production of family films in Asia has accelerated in recent years. Growth in China's independent animation sector owes a great deal to mechanisms of state support. The Shanghai Animation Film Studio, founded in 1957, was at its peak between the 1960s and the 1980s, when its films exhibited 'very high degrees of aesthetics and experimentation, while also taking on national characteristics, employing Chinese artistic techniques, and adapting stories from China's literature, folklore, and proverbs' (Lent and Xu 2010: 116). Until the mid-1990s animation in China was produced by a handful of state-owned studios and distributed by the China Film Distribution and Exhibition Corporation Company. However, in 2000, animation was officially defined as an industry, and in 2001, as Shaopeng Chen (2016) observes, 'the state decided to develop it in the long term as a part of the national economy'. By 2006, there were more than 5,000 animation studios in China, with almost 500 universities run-ning established animation programmes (Lent and Xu 2010: 121–22).

The vast majority of this animation is made for television, but China has also made strides in the production of big-budget, animated family films. *Lotus Lantern* (Guang Xi Chang, 1999), four years in the making, grossed 29 million Yuan domestically, outperforming Disney's *Mulan* (Tony Bancroft and Barry Cook, 1998) in China. But there are two major impedi-ments to the global success of Chinese feature animation. Firstly, it bears strong aesthetic similarities to Japanese anime. Secondly, while there is a reliable outlet for Chinese made-for-TV animation – much of which is produced for US programmes – feature films struggle to compete in the global marketplace. Releases such as *Kuiba* (Wang Chuan, 2011) and *The Tibetan Dog* (Masayuki Kojima, 2011) performed disastrously at the box office. However, there are signs that the situation is beginning to change. *Monkey King: Hero is Back* (Tian Xiaopeng, 2015), which was part-financed through a Crowdfunding campaign, grossed around one billion Yuan (just over US $150 million), and has been dubbed into English (Shaopeng 2016). It was also the highest-grossing animated film in China until the release of the Hollywood film, *Zootopia* (Byron Howard and Rich Moore, 2016). Such initiatives represent an alternative to co-productions such as Disney's *The Secret of the Magic Gourd* (Frankie Chung, 2007) and Oriental DreamWorks's *Kung Fu Panda 3*.

In China and India, the size of the domestic market is such that there is less need to conform to transnational narrative and aesthetic styles. Several major Indian family-oriented blockbusters fuse Hollywood fantasy tropes with 'Bollywood' conventions. The story and iconography of *Koi... Mil Gaya* (Rakesh Roshan, 2003) borrow explicitly from Spielberg's *Close Encounters of the Third Kind* and *E.T.* while retaining Bollywood character-istics of melodrama and diegetic song-and-dance sequences. Its sequel, *Krrish* (Rakesh Roshan, 2006), is a Bollywood analogue of the recent Hollywood cycle of CGI superhero movies. Although these films have a siz-able secondary market amongst Indian diasporas, they are primarily geared towards domestic audiences, as are animated films such as *Hanuman* (V. G. Samant and Milind Ukey, 2005), the country's first animated fea-ture, which is based on stories of one of the Hindu gods from the ancient Sanskrit epic, the *Ramayana*. Perhaps because of its well-established national style of cinema, India has proven difficult for Hollywood to crack.

Disney, having produced a succession of under-performing films under the UTV banner, including *Arjun: The Warrior Prince* (Arnab Chaudhuri, 2012), withdrew from the local market in late 2016.

Whilst *Koi...Mil Gaya* and *Krrish* are best described as 'family films', attempting to mobilise mass audiences of all ages, India still has a fertile tradition in child-centred narratives. While many of these films are wholesome, naturalistic morality tales, others address complex social issues under a cloak of innocuousness. In the CFSI's ecologically-themed *Xang Xang Klang* (Col Kapoor, 2010), an alien being takes the form of a human boy in order to determine whether the planet, overrun by pollution, should be destroyed. Ultimately, he decides to postpone the annihilation of the Earth to give humanity time to restore it to 'full health'. In the independent film, *Jalpari: The Desert Mermaid* (Nila Madhab Panda, 2012), two children, a brother and sister, uncover the illegal practicing of female foeticide – a hugely taboo issue in Indian society – in a rural community. Although these films are very different tonally, they share a view of children as innocent but perspicacious observers of adult society and its fallibilities.

The CFSI is currently in a period of transition. While it continues to receive government funding through the Ministry of Information and Broadcasting, it has attempted to monetise its distribution channels. In 2012, it partnered with commercial exhibition chains to distribute CFSI films in cinemas. *Gattu* (Rajan Khosa, 2012) was the first of the Society's films to receive commercial theatrical release, and it was also distributed to schools for commercial screenings ('Children's Film Society India'). CFSI Chief Executive Shravan Kumar envisaged that an 'aggressive' approach to marketing and distribution would yield a 50–60 per cent increase in revenues (ibid.). In late 2015, the CFSI sold the distribution rights to its entire catalogue of films to a commercial distributor, Ultra Media & Entertainment (Levine 2015). Most significantly, in January 2016 the CFSI announced plans to co-produce films with commercial partners. Such films will centre on children but feature adult stars to broaden the appeal to older audiences, following the example of *Like Stars on Earth* (*Taare Zameen Par*, Aamir Khan, 2007), a child-oriented film produced by, and co-starring, Bollywood superstar Aamir Khan. Budgets, however, remain low; in early 2016, the Society allocated 10 crore – just over $1 million – towards five or six films. More notably, the CFSI has outsourced responsibility for the production, marketing and distribution of its co-productions to its commercial partner.

Its attempts to establish a commercial footing have taken several other forms, including DVD sales, tie-ups with multiplex chains, and both free and paid screenings in schools. In addition, the Society has been acquiring the rights to international films, dubbing them into Indian dialects and recouping money through screenings and home video sales ('CFSI to Make 5–6 Children's Films'). CFSI chairman Mukesh Khanna explained the new policies by remarking: 'If we do not release the movies in theatre[s], [they] will never reach [...] children' ('There's No Good Content').

In India and elsewhere, film festivals remain vital to the distribution of children's films worldwide. However, their limitations as a forum for transnational cultural exchange are obvious: in 2007 Günther Kinstler, a former organiser of the Frankfurt International Film Festival, observed that while more children's film festivals exist than ever before, 'the chances for (a film] to find its way to young audiences in cinemas or on TV screens have decreased to a remarkable degree' (Rössler et al. 2009: 22). The ongoing reliance on festivals reflects the oligopolistic nature of international multimedia distribution – an oligopoly that global digital connectivity has failed to break. One alternative is the independent 'micro-budget' film, typically privately financed, shot with basic equipment, and distributed online. *Who Killed Nelson Nutmeg?* (Tim Clague and Danny Stack, 2015), a British children's film produced for approximately £300,000, premiered at the BFI London Film Festival in October 2015 and has subsequently been made available on video-on-demand (VOD) systems. Whether VOD represents a viable long-term alternative to theatrical distribution channels remains to be seen. Since promotional campaigns for big-budget films typically run into the tens or hundreds of million dollars, the multinational conglomerates – with their deep pockets – hold a significant competitive advantage.

Mainstream family films operate within a larger field of multimedia entertainment. Disney's revived *Star Wars* trilogy (2015–), produced by J. J. Abrams, is part of a franchise that encompasses TV shows, theme park rides, books, home video, comic books, video games and tie-ins with toy and clothes manufacturers and restaurants. The intrinsic value of the films is immense: *Star Wars: The Force Awakens*, released in 2015, grossed more than $2 billion. But their value in sustaining and invigorating the *Star Wars* franchise may be greater still. The current film trilogy would not exist but for the fact that the *Star Wars* brand has been kept alive in the years between film instalments. Equally, franchises require new content to keep the brand profitable in the longer-term. Essentially, the old industry maxim that 'content is king' may stand; but brands, as one Universal executive put it, 'are the new stars' (Graser 2009).

With post-1990s Hollywood family entertainment, we can discuss individual film cycles in context of the wider brand, rather than vice versa. In some cases, such as Disney's *Pirates of the Caribbean* (theme park ride) and DreamWorks's *Transformers* (toy line) series, the film adaptation is less a self-contained artistic statement than an extension of a family-oriented multimedia brand into a new medium – one that avails the potential for further synergistic outlets. Film, in this context, retains its uniqueness in a crowded market, since the global theatrical audience for family films is still disproportionately high, and the cost of movie tickets is far greater than digitally streaming multimedia content at home.

As we have seen, transnational trends have implications for film content. One tendency when addressing a broad international audience is to flatten strong cultural markers. A contrary tendency is that of local resistance to globalisation, leading to revanchist attempts – particularly in cultures where US 'cultural imperialism' is most strongly felt – to reassert local and national specificities. Yet it is probable that the biggest impact of cultural and economic transnationalism is not in the films themselves, but rather the context in which they are consumed. Independent children's films not operating within the multimedia franchise model may be approached without preconceptions or prior knowledge, but in the multimedia, transnational family entertainment arena, film is rarely an independent entity. Films derived from 'pre-texts' such as books, comics, television shows or other source material are likely to be consumed in conjunction with other iterations of the brand. The most important implication is that while there are many *textual* similarities between contemporary children's films and family films – remembering the overarching conventions of children's cinema discussed in Chapter 1 – viewers' perceptions and experiences of them are likely to be very different.

4   POSTSCRIPT

A single volume of this length – or, indeed, of *any* practical length – cannot fully do justice to the children's film in all its diversity. It is a form that encompasses well over 100 years of production in multiple languages, crossing boundaries of politics, aesthetics, genre, nation and cultural identity. However, throughout this book I have maintained that there are larger patterns within the various national and regional traditions of children's cinema. The vast majority of films work to inculcate ideologically 'correct' moral and behavioural practices, upholding social and behavioural norms. They foreground real or symbolic child figures and their experiences of the world, downplay strongly 'adult' situations (such as explicit violence or sex), negate ambiguity, and provide moral and emotional uplift. These conventions are not inviolable. As we have seen, for instance, various children's films articulate implicit or explicit resistance to the ideological status quo. However, obvious violations, such as the 'unhappy endings' of films like *My Girl* and *Old Yeller*, tend to be noticed and commented on. But it is important to emphasise that children's film is constantly evolving. Changing attitudes to childhood (and adulthood) underpin the more liberal treatment of violence and sexuality in Western cinemas, as well as greater degrees of moral and narrative ambiguity. We recognise children's films through their adherence to these broad conventions, but also by contextual discourses such as advertisements, film ratings and censorship restrictions, critical responses, merchandising strategies and exhibition patterns. Children's films are manufactured via a complex interaction between these textual and non-textual mechanisms.

In the early twentieth century, children's cinema developed in two partly intersecting, partly discrete traditions, the first primarily non-commercial and state-funded, and the second primarily commercial. With recent trends towards industrial transnationalism and mixed-economy funding models, these distinctions are no longer so rigid. However, they remain the primary determinants of generic identity between the overlapping 'children's film' and 'family film' categories. A broad, but not absolute, movement has occurred from the localism and nationalism of the films examined in Chapter 3 to the transnationalism of the post-1980s children's and family films discussed in Chapter 4. The explicit, paternalistic view of children as requiring moral guidance has partly been displaced. Relatedly, as a consequence of lowering of trade barriers, many national traditions of children's cinema have weakened in the face of Hollywood competition and the perennial lack of funding. One of the defining issues in studying contemporary children's cinema is how national and/or regional traditions adapt to the cultural and economic implications of 'globalisation'.

Changing cultural and industrial contexts promote variations in style and narrative. The organisational infrastructure of the Hollywood studio system has always regulated and standardised production based on social and psychological norms and perceived patterns of consumer behaviour. Post-1970s multimedia conglomeration and multimedia franchising have intensified this standardisation. Despite liberalising attitudes to class, race, gender and sexuality, Hollywood family films are founded on pleasurable repetitions of established formulae. If one examines children's cinema through the narrow lens of mainstream Hollywood, it is easy to assume, *prima facie* – as some critics (e.g. Neff 1996; Mallan 2000) have done – that the genre is inherently conservative. However, at the time of writing, children's cinema may be the most diverse and creative it has ever been. Internationally, films are made in a wide variety of aesthetic and generic styles. Many of them deal with serious issues; some are vehicles to question or to protest against dominant social practices. Indeed, the genre's apparent conservatism has allowed some filmmakers to deal with politically sensitive issues in ways that would be impossible in mainstream cinema. The specificity of children's cinema lies partially in its ability to offer a unique perspective (the child's point-of-view) on culture and society under a cloak of innocence.

Another important development in the production and reception of children's film in many countries is that adults' consumption of them is now a widely accepted phenomenon, no longer subject to stigmatisation. In part, this is a result of the commercialisation of children's media and its assimilation into the cultural mainstream. State-funded films were often intended exclusively for children and, being exhibited in schools and children's matinees, were inaccessible to adults. In contrast, commercial films purposely address mixed audiences of children and adults. This has led to a broad, and still under-addressed, phenomenon where child-oriented films are no longer regarded exclusively, or even primarily, as belonging to children. Whether this trend is part of a larger 'infantilisation' of Western popular culture or an 'adultification' of children's cinema is a matter of considerable wider debate. Such ambiguities reveal a need for ethnographic research that explores habits of consumption at local, national and international levels. Who really watches children's films, and what do people do with their experiences of them? Of course, children's film is such a vast entity that any research, no matter how wide-ranging, could contribute only a small piece of a much larger puzzle.

Children's cinema may be governed by broad, structuring conventions, but remains pluralistic in the themes and ideologies it explores, in its stylistic and aesthetic range, and in the audiences it mobilises. Children's films are radical and conservative; they are escapist and didactic; they are formally conventional and stylistically innovative. The international popularity of the genre underlines the fact that children's film is not some other realm, separated from (or inferior to) a more legitimate 'adult' cinema. Nevertheless, it is a form of popular culture that carries its own specific structures and meanings which demand serious analysis. Because of its didactic imperative, children's cinema is also a profound expression of individual and collective identity – the codes, values, customs and norms that represent society's claim to civilisation.

SELECT FILMOGRAPHY

Note: In instances where films have not received an English-language release, or are not widely known by their English titles, the original title has been retained.

5,000 Fingers of Dr. T. Dir. Roy Rowland. Columbia: 1953.

Adventures of Goopy and Bagha, The. Dir. Satyajit Ray. Purnima Pictures: 1969.

Alesha Popovich i Tugarin Zmei. Dir. Konstatin Bronzit. Melnitsa: 2004.

Arjun: The Warrior Prince. Dir. Arnab Chaudhuri. UTV: 2012.

Arthur and the Invisibles. Dir. Luc Besson. MGM: 2006.

Asterix and Obelix vs. Caesar. Dir. Claude Zidi. StudioCanal: 1999.

Asterix & Obelix: Mission Cleopatra. Dir. Alain Chabat. StudioCanal: 2002.

Atmospheric Layer Vanishes, The. Dir. Feng Xiaoning. Children's Film Studio: 1990.

Babe. Dir. Chris Noonan. Universal: 1995.

Battle for Billy's Pond, The. Dir. Harley Cokeliss. Children's Film Foundation: 1976.

Charandas Chor. Dir. Shyam Benegal. Children's Film Society, India: 1975.

Chicken Feather Letter. Dir. Shi Hui. Shanghai Film Studio: 1954.

Chicken Run. Dirs. Nick Park and Peter Lord. Aardman: 2000.

Chitty Chitty Bang Bang. Dir. Ken Hughes. United Artists: 1968.

Cinderella. Dir. Georges Méliès. Star Film Company: 1899.

Cinderella. Dirs. Nadezhda Kosheverova and Mikhail Shapiro. LenFilm: 1947.

Curse of the Were-Rabbit, The. Dirs. Nick Park and Steve Box. Aardman: 2005.

Ditte, Child of Man. Dir. Bjarne Henning-Jensen. Nordisk Film: 1946.

Dobrynia Nikitych i Zmei Gorynych. Dir. Ilia Maksimov. Melnitsa: 2006.

Emil and the Detectives. Dir. Gerhard Lamprecht. UFA: 1931.

Emperor's Nightingale, The. Dir. Jirí Trnka. Ceskoslovenský Státní Film: 1949.

E.T.: The Extra Terrestrial. Dir. Steven Spielberg. Universal: 1982.

Fiddlesticks. Dir. Veit Helmer. Veit Helmer Filmproduktion: 2014.

Frozen. Dirs. Chris Buck and Jennifer Lee. Disney: 2013.

Hanuman. Dirs. V. G. Samant and Milind Ukey. Percept Picture Company: 2005.

Harry Potter and the Philosopher's Stone. Dir. Chris Columbus. Warner Bros.: 2001.

Harry Potter and the Deathly Hallows, Part 2. Dir. David Yates. Warner Bros.: 2011.

Hue and Cry. Dir. Charles Crichton. Ealing Studios: 1947.

Humpbacked Horse, The. Dir. Ivan Ivanov-Vano. Soiuzmul'tfilm: 1947.

Ilia Muromets i Solovei Razboinik. Dir. Vladimir Toropchin. Melnitsa: 2007.

Jaldeep. Dir. Kedar Sharma. Children's Film Society, India: 1956.

Jalpari: The Desert Mermaid. Dir. Nila Madhab Panda. Ultra Distributors: 2012.

Keshu. Dir. Sivan. Children's Film Society, India: 2009.

Kidz in Da Hood. Dirs. Catti Edfeldt and Ylva Gustavsson. Sonet Film: 2006.

Kingdom of Diamonds. Dir. Satyajit Ray. Government of West Bengal: 1980.

Koi...Mil Gaya. Dir. Rakesh Roshan. Film Kraft: 2003.

Krrish. Dir. Rakesh Roshan. Film Kraft: 2006.

Kung Fu Panda 3. Dirs. Jennifer Yuh Nelson and Alessandro Carloni. Fox: 2016.

L'Arroseur arrosé. Dir. Louis Lumière. Lumière: 1895.

Like Stars on Earth. Dir. Aamir Khan. PVR Pictures: 2007.

Little Women. Dir. George Cukor. RKO: 1933.

Lion King, The. Dirs. Roger Allers and Rob Minkoff. Disney: 1994.

Maleficent. Dir. Robert Stromberg. Disney: 2014.

Mary Poppins. Dir. Robert Stevenson. Disney: 1964.

Meet Me in St. Louis. Dir. Vincente Minnelli. MGM: 1944.

Midsummer Night's Dream, A. Dir. Jirí Trnka. Ceskoslovenský Státní Film: 1959.

Monkey King: Hero is Back. Dir. Tian Xiaopeng. Beijing Weiyingshidai: 2015.
Moor and the Ravens of London. Dir. Helmut Dziuba. DEFA: 1969.
Mrs. Doubtfire. Dir. Chris Columbus. Twentieth Century Fox: 1993.
Old Czech Legends. Dir. Jirí Trnka. Ceskoslovenský Státní Film: 1953.
Paddington. Dir. Paul King. Studio Canal: 2014.
ParaNorman. Dir. Chris Butler and Sam Fell. Universal: 2012.
Railway Children, The. Dir Lionel Jeffries. EMI: 1970.
Red Balloon, The. Dir. Albert Lamorisse. Films Montsouris: 1956.
Rubber Tarzan. Dir. Søren Kragh-Jacobsen. Metronome Productions: 1981.
Shaun the Sheep Movie. Dirs. Richard Starzak and Mark Burton. Aardman:
    2015.
Shrek. Dirs. Andrew Adamson and Vicky Jenson. DreamWorks: 2001.
Sleeping Beauty. Dir. Walter Beck. DEFA: 1971.
Snowman, The. Dir. Dianne Jackson. TVC: 1982.
Snow White and the Seven Dwarfs. Dir. David Hand. Disney: 1937.
Snow White. Dir. Gottfried Kolditz. DEFA: 1961.
Sparkling Red Star. Dirs. Li Jun and Li Ang. August First Film Studio: 1974.
Star Wars. Dir. George Lucas. Twentieth Century Fox: 1977.
Star Wars: The Force Awakens. Dir. J. J. Abrams. Disney: 2015.
Taare Zameen Par. Dir. Aamir Khan. UTV: 2007.
Tarka the Otter. Dir. David Cobham. Tor Films Limited: 1979.
Terkel in Trouble. Dirs. Kresten Vestsbjerg Andersen et al. Nordisk Film:
    2004.
Thief of Bagdad, The. Dirs. Michael Powell et al. London Films: 1940.
Toy Story. Dir. John Lasseter. Disney: 1995.
Treasure Island. Dir. Vladimir Vaynshtok. Gorky: 1938.
Tri Bogatyria i Shamakhanskaia Tsaritsa. Dir. Sergei Glezin. Melnitsa: 2010.
We Shall Overcome. Dir. Niels Arden Oplev. Zentropa: 2006.
Where is the Friend's Home? Dir. Abbas Kiarostami. Kanoon: 1987.
Willy Wonka and the Chocolate Factory. Dir. Mel Stuart. Warner Bros.: 1971.
Wizard of Oz, The. Dir. Victor Fleming. MGM: 1939.
Xang Xang Klang. Dir. Col Kapoor. Children's Film Society, India: 2010.

SELECT BIBLIOGRAPHY

Agrawal, S. P. and J. C. Aggarwal (eds). *Nehru on Social Issues* (New Delhi: Askok Kumar Mittal, 1989).

Allen, Robert C. 'Home Alone Together: Hollywood and the "Family Film"' in Melvyn Stokes and Richard Maltby (eds), *Identifying Hollywood's Audiences: Cultural Identity and the Movies* (London: British Film Institute, 1999), pp. 109–34.

Altman, Rick. 'A Semantic/Syntactic Approach to Film Genre' in Barry Keith Grant (ed.), *Film Genre Reader III* (Austin: University of Texas Press, 2003), pp. 27–41.

Austin, Guy. *Contemporary French Cinema: An Introduction*, 2nd edition (Manchester: Manchester University Press, 2008).

Babington, Bruce. '"To Catch a Star on your Fingertips": Diagnosing the Medical Biopic from *The Story of Louis Pasteur* to Freud' in Graeme Harper and Andrew Moor (eds), *Signs of Life: Medicine and Cinema* (London and New York: Wallflower, 2005), pp. 120–31.

'Bagdad Also Will Have Commercial Licensing Hookup'. *Variety*, 27 December 1939, p. 8.

Balina, Marina and Birgit Beumers. '"To Catch Up and Overtake Disney"? Soviet and Post-Soviet Fairy-Tale Films' in Jack Zipes, Pauline Greenhill and Kendra Magnus-Johnston (eds), *Fairy-Tale Films Beyond Disney: International Perspectives* (New York: Routledge, 2016), pp. 124–38.

Barefoot, Guy. 'Who Watched That Masked Man: Hollywood's Serial Audiences in the 1930s'. *The Historical Journal of Film, Radio and Television*, vol. 31, no. 3 (2011), pp. 167–90.

Bazalgette, Cary and Terry Staples. 'Unshrinking the Kids: Children's Cinema and the Family Film' in Cary Bazalgette and David Buckingham (eds), *In Front of the Children* (London: British Film Institute, 1995), pp. 92–108.

Beeler, Karin and Stan Beeler (eds). *Children's Film in the Digital Age: Essays on Audience. Adaptation and Consumer Culture* (Jefferson, N.C.: McFarland, 2015).

Blessing, Benita. 'DEFA Children's Films: Not Just for Children' in Marc Silberman and Henning Wrage (eds), *DEFA at the Crossroads of East German and International Film Culture* (Berlin: DeGruyter, 2014), pp. 243–62.

Blessing, Benita. '"Films to Give Kids Courage!": Children's Films in the German Democratic Republic' in Noel Brown and Bruce Babington (eds), *Family Films in Global Cinema: The World Beyond Disney* (London and New York: I.B. Tauris, 2015), pp. 155–70.

Boero, Davide. *All'ombra del proiettore: il cinema per ragazzi nell'Italia del dopoguerra* (Macerata: EUM, 2013).

Booker, M. Keith. *Disney, Pixar, and the Hidden Messages of Children's Films* (California: Praeger, 2010).

Brown, Noel. *The Hollywood Family Film: A History, from Shirley Temple to Harry Potter* (London and New York: I.B. Tauris, 2012).

Brown, Noel. 'The "Family" Film, and the Tensions Between Popular and Academic Interpretations of Genre'. *Trespassing Journal: An Online Journal of Trespassing Art, Science and Philosophy*, no. 2 (2013a), pp. 22–35.

Brown, Noel. '"A New Movie-Going Public": 1930s Hollywood and the Emergence of the "Family" Film'. *The Historical Journal of Film, Radio and Television*, vol. 33, no. 1 (2013b), pp. 1–23.

Brown, Noel. '"Family" Entertainment and Contemporary Hollywood Cinema'. *Scope: An Online Journal of Film and Television Studies*, no. 25 (2013c), pp. 1–22.

Brown, Noel. 'Asterix and Obelix vs. Hollywood: A Pan-European Entertainment Franchise for the "Family" Audience' in Karin Beeler and Stan Beeler (eds), *Children's Film in the Digital Age: Essays on Audience, Adaptation and Consumer Culture* (Jefferson, N.C.: McFarland, 2015a), pp. 49–61.

Brown, Noel. 'Individualism and National Identity in Disney's Early British

Films'. *Journal of Popular Film and Television*, vol. 43, no. 4 (2015b), pp. 188–200.

Brown, Noel. *British Children's Cinema: From The Thief of Bagdad to Wallace and Gromit* (London and New York: I.B. Tauris, 2016).

Brown, Noel and Bruce Babington (eds). *Family Films in Global Cinema: The World Beyond Disney* (London and New York: I.B. Tauris, 2015).

Brown, Noel and Bruce Babington. 'Introduction: Children's Films and Family Films' in Noel Brown and Bruce Babington (eds), *Family Films in Global Cinema: The World Beyond Disney* (London and New York: I.B. Tauris, 2015), pp. 1–16.

'Campaign Raises Oz Chicago Gross'. *Motion Picture Herald*, 2 September 1939, p. 25.

'CFSI to make 5-6 Children's Films in 2016 with Big Producers'. *The Times of India*, 11 January 2016, unpaginated.

'Children's Film Society India Targets 50%-60% Revenue Through Innovative Marketing', *DNA India.com*, 14 September 2014. ⟨http://www.dnaindia.com/entertainment/report-children-s-film-society-india-targets-50-60-revenue-through-innovative-marketing-2018579⟩ (accessed 6 December 2016).

Chrisafis, Angelique. 'UK Bids to be Player in Films for Children'. *The Guardian*, 11 October 2003, p. 7.

The Cinema: Its Present Position and Future Possibilities – Being the Report and Chief Evidence Taken by the Cinema Commission of Inquiry Instituted by the National Council of Public Morals (London: Williams and Norgate, 1917).

'Clean Films Necessary to Promote Family Values: CM'. *The Times of India*, 24 March 2012, unpaginated.

Collins, Fiona M. and Jeremy Ridgman (eds). *Turning the Page: Children's Literature in Performance and the Media* (Bern: Peter Lang, 2006).

Cook, David A. *Lost Illusions: American Cinema in the Shadow of Watergate and Vietnam, 1970–1979* (Berkeley, Los Angeles and London: University of California Press, 2000).

Cox, Carole. 'Children's Films: The Literature Connection'. *Children's Literature Association Quarterly*, vol. 7, no. 3 (1982), pp. 10–13.

Culf, Andrew, '181,000 Children Saw Horror Film', *The Guardian*, 15 December 1993, p. 2.

Cunningham, Jennifer. 'Children's Humour' in W. George Scarlett *et al.*

(eds), *Children's Play* (London and New Delhi: Sage, 2005), pp. 93-109.

Dale, Edgar. *Children's Attendance at Motion Pictures* (New York: Macmillan, 1935).

Doherty, Thomas. *Teenagers and Teenpics: The Juvenilization of American Movies in the 1950s* (Philadelphia: University of Temple Press, 2002).

Donald, Stephanie. *Public Secrets, Public Spaces: Cinema and Civility in China* (Lanham: Rowman and Littlefield, 2000).

Donald, Stephanie. *Little Friends: Children's Film and Media Culture in China* (Lanham: Rowman and Littlefield, 2005).

Donald, Stephanie Hemelryk and Kirsten Seale. 'Children's Film Culture' in Dafna Lemish (ed.), *The Routledge International Handbook of Children, Adolescents, and Media* (London and New York: Routledge, 2013), pp. 95–102.

Every Saturday Night press book (BFI).

Farber, Stephen. *The Movie Rating Game* (Washington, D.C.: Public Affairs Press, 1972).

Farrand Thorp, Margaret. *America at the Movies* (London: Faber and Faber, 1945).

Field, Mary. *Good Company: The Story of the Children's Entertainment Film Movement in Great Britain – 1943–1950* (London: Longmans Green and Co., 1952).

Freud, Sigmund. 'Delusions and Dreams in Jenson's *Gradiva*' in *Psychological Writings and Letters* (London: Continuum, 1995).

Frow, John. *Genre: The New Critical Idiom* (London: Routledge, 2005).

'A Future for British Film: It Begins with the Audience...'. Film Policy Review Panel Report (London: Department for Culture, Media and Sport, 2012).

Ganti, Tejaswini. *Bollywood: A Guide to Popular Hindi Cinema* (New York and London: Routledge, 2004).

Geer, Jennifer. 'J. M. Barrie Gets the Miramax Treatment: Finding (and Marketing) Neverland'. *Children's Literature Association Quarterly*, vol. 32, no. 3 (2007), pp. 193–212.

Goldstein, Ruth M. and Edith Zornow. *The Screen Image of Youth: Movies about Children and Adolescents* (Metuchen: Scarecrow, 1980).

Graser, Marc. 'Hollywood: Lost Boys Refound'. *Variety*, 28 September 2009, p. 1.

Grenby, M. O. (ed.). *The Cambridge Companion to Children's Literature* (Cambridge: Cambridge University Press, 2009).

Gritten, David. 'Film on Friday'. *The Daily Telegraph*, 28 October 2005, p. 27.

Gunning, Tom. 'The Cinema of Attractions: Early Cinema, its Spectator, and the Avant Garde' in Thomas Elsaesser (ed.), *Early Cinema: Space Frame Narrative* (London: British Film Institute, 1990), pp. 56–62.

Hall, Mordaunt. 'A German Juvenile Film'. *The New York Times*, 21 December 1931, p. 28.

Harmetz, Aljean. *The Making of the Wizard of Oz* (New York: Alfred A. Knopf, 1977).

Hermans, Gert, Wendy Koops, and Nina Cetinic. 'It Is Time For a New Approach?', *ECFA Journal*, no. 4 (December 2008), pp. 1–3.

Jackson, Kathy Merlock. *Images of Children in American Film: A Sociocultural Analysis* (London: Scarecrow Press, 1986).

Jackson, Kathy Merlock (ed.). *Walt Disney: Conversations* (Jackson: University Press of Mississippi, 2006).

Jowett, Garth. *Film: The Democratic Art* (Boston, Toronto: Little, Brown and Company, 1976).

'Juvenile Books for Oz, Gulliver and Pinocchio'. *Film Daily*, 25 August 1939, p. 7.

Kaspersen, Flemming. 'Humour, Gravity and Fantasy: Sixty Years of Danish Films for Children'. *Films for Children and Young People: The Danish Experience* (2007), pp. 3–4. ‹http://www.dfi.dk/NR/rdonlyres/BE741725-2B58-47D1-BEA5-A703E1B353F1/0/Rio2007folderpdf.pdf› (accessed 23/04/2012).

Kasson, John F. 'Behind Shirley Temple's Smile: Children, Emotional Labour, and the Great Depression' in James W. Cook, Lawrence B. Glickman and Michael O'Malley (eds), *The Cultural Turn in U.S. History: Past, Present, and Future* (Chicago and London: The University of Chicago Press, 2008), pp. 185–216.

Kesterton, Barbara. 'The Social and Emotional Effects of the Recreational Film on Adolescents of 13 and 14 Years of Age in the West Bromwich Area'. PhD thesis submitted to The University of Birmingham, 1948.

Kirkland, Ewan. 'The Politics of Children's Cinema'. PhD thesis submitted to the University of Sussex (2004).

Kleber, Reinhard. 'Original Children's Films Urgently Wanted'. *Goethe-Institut*, January 2016, unpaginated.

Kononenko, Natalie. 'Post-Soviet Parody: Can Family Films about Russian

Heroes Be Funny?' in Noel Brown and Bruce Babington (eds), *Family Films in Global Cinema: The World Beyond Disney* (London and New York: I.B. Tauris, 2015), pp. 171–85.

Koszarski, Richard. *An Evening's Entertainment: The Age of the Silent Feature Picture* (Berkeley: University of California Press, 1990).

Krämer, Peter. 'Would You Take Your Child to See This Film?: The Cultural and Social Work of the Family Adventure Movie', in Steve Neale and Murray Smith (eds), *Contemporary Hollywood Cinema* (London: Routledge, 1998), pp. 294–311.

Krämer, Peter. '"The Best Disney Film Disney Never Made": Children's Films and The Family Audience in American Cinema since the 1960s', in Steve Neale (ed.), *Genre and Contemporary Hollywood* (London: British Film Institute, 2002), pp. 185–200.

Krämer, Peter. '"It's Aimed at Kids – The Kid in Everybody': George Lucas, *Star Wars* and Children's Entertainment' in Yvonne Tasker (ed.), *Action and Adventure Cinema* (London and New York: Routledge, 2004), pp. 358–70.

Krämer, Peter. '"A film specially suitable for children": The Marketing and Reception of *2001: A Space Odyssey* (1968)' in Noel Brown and Bruce Babington (eds), *Family Films in Global Cinema: The World Beyond Disney* (London and New York: I.B. Tauris, 2015), pp. 37–52.

Kümmerling-Meibauer, Bettina. 'Introduction: New Perspectives in Children's Film Studies'. *Journal of Educational Media, Memory, and Society*, vol. 8, no. 2 (2013), pp. 39–44.

Lathey, Gillian. '"What a Funny Name!": Cultural Transition in Versions of Erich Kästner's *Emil and the Detectives*' in Fiona M. Collins and Jeremy Ridgman (eds), *Turning the Page: Children's Literature in Performance and the Media* (Bern: Peter Lang, 2004), pp. 115–32.

Lawrence, Will. 'Sex, Potions and Rock 'n' Roll'. *The Daily Telegraph*, 3 July 2009, p. 29.

Lejeune, C. A. 'The Pictures: A Boys' Film'. *The Observer*, 19 March 1933, p. 14.

Lent, John A. and Ying Xu. 'Chinese Animation Film: From Experimentation to Digitalisation' in Ying Zhu and Stanley Rossen (eds), *Art, Politics and Commerce in Chinese Cinema* (Hong Kong: Hong Kong University Press, 2010), pp. 111–25.

Levine, Sydney. 'Ultra Media Acquires Entire Collection from Children's

Film Society, India for Global Distribution'. *IndieWire*, 27 December 2015. ‹http://www.indiewire.com/2015/12/ultra-media-acquires-entire-collection-from-childrens-film-society-india-for-global-distribution-168311/› (accessed 6 December 2016).

Little Women press book (BFI).

Lury, Karen. *The Child in Film: Tears, Fears and Fairytales* (London and New York: I.B. Tauris, 2010).

Mallan, Kerry M. 'Witches, Bitches and Femme Fatales: Viewing the Female Grotesque in Children's Film'. *Papers: Explorations into Children's Literature*, vol. 10, no. 1 (2000), pp. 26–35.

'Mayer, Schary, Rodgers Star as MGM Winds Big Sales Meet'. *Variety*, 11 February 1949, p. 3.

Meet Me in St. Louis press book (BFI).

'MGM Wins Most Blue Ribbons in 20 Years of These Awards'. *Boxoffice*, 10 January 1953, p. 11.

Miller Mitchell, Alice. *Children and Movies* (Chicago: University of Chicago Press, 1929).

Morris, Timothy. *You're Only Young Twice: Children's Literature and Film* (Urbana: University of Illinois Press, 2000).

'MPAA Theatrical Market Statistics 2013'. Motion Picture Association of America (2014).

'MPAA Theatrical Market Statistics 2014'. Motion Picture Association of America (2015).

Mulay, Vijara. 'Where are the Children's Films?'. *Vidura*, 8 December 1981, unpaginated.

Murphy, Ryan. 'The Kids are All Right'. *Entertainment Weekly*, 16 April 1993, unpaginated.

Napier, Susan J. *Animé from Akira to Howl's Moving Castle: Experiencing Contemporary Japanese Animation*, 2nd edn. (New York: Palgrave Macmillan, 2005).

Neale, Steve. *Genre and Hollywood* (London: Routledge, 2000).

Neff, Heather. 'Strange Faces in the Mirror: The Ethics of Diversity in Children's Films'. *The Lion and the Unicorn*, vol. 20, no. 1 (1996), pp. 50–65.

'New plan to put Warners in Family way'. *Variety*, 9 December 1991, pp. 1, 3.

Newton, Michael. 'Til I'm Grown: Reading Children's Films; Reading Walt Disney's *The Jungle Book*' in Fiona M. Collins and Jeremy Ridgman (eds), *Turning the Page: Children's Literature in Performance and the Media* (Bern: Peter Lang, 2006), pp. 17–38.

O'Connor, Joanne. 'Wizard! Harry Saves Tour Industry'. *The Observer*, 27 April 2003, p. E20.

Ortiz Ramos, José Mário. *Cinema, Televisão e Publicidade: Cultura Popular de Massa no Brasil dos Anos 1970–1980* (São Paulo: Annablume, 2004).

Ou, Mirian and Alessandro Constantino Gamo. 'Brazilian Children's Cinema in the 1990s: Tensions Between the National-Popular and the International-Popular' in Noel Brown and Bruce Babington (eds), *Family Films in Global Cinema: The World Beyond Disney* (London and New York: I.B. Tauris, 2015), pp. 207–22.

'Oz'. *Film Daily*, 11 August 1939, pp. 4–5.

Pallant, Chris. *Demystifying Disney: A History of Disney Feature Animation* (London: Continuum, 2011).

Parry, Becky. *Children, Film and Literacy* (Basingstoke: Palgrave Macmillan, 2013).

Pendakur, Manjunath. 'India's National Film Policy: Shifting Currents in the 1990s' in Albert Moran (ed.), *Film Policy: International, National and Regional Perspectives* (London and New York: Routledge, 1996), pp. 145–68.

Pontieri, Laura. *Soviet Animation and the Thaw of the 1960s: Not Only for Children* (Hampshire: John Libbey, 2013).

'Production of "Snow White" Marks New Film Epoch'. *The Motion Picture and the Family*, 15 January 1938, p. 1.

Prokhorev, Alexander. 'Arresting Development: A Brief History of Soviet Cinema for Children and Adolescents' in Marina Balina and Larissa Rudova (eds), *Russian Children's Literature and Culture* (New York: Routledge, 2008), pp. 129–52.

Rajadhyaksha, Ashish. 'Satyajit Ray' in Geoffrey Nowell-Smith (ed.), *The Oxford History of World Cinema* (Oxford: Oxford University Press, 1996), pp. 682–83.

Riding, Alan. 'French Comic Book Heroes Battle Hollywood's Hordes'. *The New York Times*, 10 February 1999, p. E5.

Robinson, Andrew, *Satyajit Ray: The Inner Eye* (London: Deutsch, 1989).

Rössler, Patrick, Kathleen Arendt, Anja Kalch and Franziska Spitzner. 'Children's Film in Europe: A Literature Review' (Erfurt: University of Erfurt, 2009).

Roychoudhuri, Upendrakishore (ed.). *Goopy Gyne Bagha Byne and Other Stories* (London: Penguin, 2015).

Schäfer, Horst. *Kindheit und Film: Geschichte, Themen und Perspektiven des Kinderfilms in Deutschland* (Konstanz: UVK Verlagsgesellschaft, 2009).

Scheur, Philip K. 'Films for Children Urged by Radnitz', *The Los Angeles Times*, 14 October 1963, p. D9.

Schöffel, Reinhold T. 'ECFA's Survey on Children's Film Distribution in Europe', *ECFA Journal*, March 2008. ‹http://www.ecfaweb.org/projects/distribution/statistics.htm› (accessed 24 November 2016).

Schickel, Richard. *The Disney Version* (Chicago: Elephant Paperback, 1997).

'Serials Making Comeback'. *Boxoffice*, 3 July 1937, p. 24.

Shaopeng Chen. 'Industrial Transformation and Aesthetic Exploration: China's New Generation Cinema Animation'. Unpublished paper presented at the *Theorising the Popular* conference, Liverpool Hope University, June 2016.

Shaw, Deborah. 'Deconstructing and Reconstructing Transnational Cinema' in Stephanie Dennison (ed.), *Contemporary Hispanic Cinema: Interrogating the Transnational in Spanish and Latin American Film* (Woodbridge: Tamesis, 2013), pp. 47–66.

'Showmen's Reviews'. *Motion Picture Herald*, 23 November 1935, p. 70.

Simonton, Dean Keith, Lauren Elizabeth Skidmore, and James C. Kaufman. 'Mature Cinematic Content for Immature Minds: "Pushing the Envelope" vs. "Toning it Down" in Family Films', *Empirical Studies of the Arts*, vol. 30, no. 2 (2012), pp. 143–66.

Sinyard, Neil. *Children in the Movies* (London: B. T. Batsford, 1992).

Skupa, Lukáš. 'Children's Films: Between Education, Art and Industry' in Lars Karl and Pavel Skopal (eds), *Cinema in Service of the State: Perspectives on Film Culture in the GDR and Czechoslovakia, 1945–1960* (New York: Bergahn, 2015), pp. 205–26.

Smith, Michelle R. 'Transformers Movie Marketing for Kids Criticised'. *Thestar.com*, 9 January 2008. ‹https://www.thestar.com/entertainment/2008/01/09/transformer_movie_marketing_for_kids_criticized.html› (accessed 13 July 2016).

Smoodin, Eric. *Animating Culture: Hollywood Cartoons in the Sound Era* (Oxford: Roundhouse Publishing, 1993).

Soila, Tytti. 'Elvis! Elvis' in *The Cinema of Scandinavia* (London: Wallflower, 2005), pp. 171–80.

Spear, Ivan. 'A Fairy Tale to Glowing Life upon the Screen', *Boxoffice*, 25 December 1937, p. 18.

Sporberg, Mrs. William Dick. 'A Clubwoman Chats on Films for the Family', *The Motion Picture and the Family*, 15 January 1937, pp. 3–4.

Staples, Terry. *All Pals Together: The Story of Children's Cinema* (Edinburgh: Edinburgh University Press, 1997).

Stedman, Raymond William. *The Serials: Suspense and Drama by Instalment* (Norman: University of Oklahoma Press, 1971).

Stephens, John and Robyn McCallum. *Retelling Stories, Framing Culture: Traditional Story and Metanarratives in Children's Literature* (New York: Garland, 1998).

Storck, Henri. *The Entertainment Film for Juvenile Audiences* (Paris: UNESCO, 1950).

'There's No Good Content for Kids in India: Mukesh Khanna'. *The Indian Express*, 9 November 2016, unpaginated.

Ting He. 'American Family Entertainment and the Only Child Generation in Contemporary Urban China'. PhD thesis submitted to the University of East Anglia (2013).

Vanginderhuysen, Felix. 'Focus on the Distribution of Films for Children in Europe'. *ECFA Journal*, December 2005. ‹http://www.ecfaweb.org/projects/survey/doco.htm› (accessed 24 November 2016).

Vivarelli, Nick. 'Scandi Markets Drive Kidpic Biz: Laws Set Aside Coin for Children's Films', *Variety*, 5 February 2007, p. 60.

Wall, Barbara. *The Narrator's Voice: The Dilemma of Children's Fiction* (New York: St. Martin's Press, 1991).

'Wallace and Gromit in Tourism Campaign'. *The Glasgow Herald*, 9 May 2013, p. 3.

'Walt Disney, UTV to Co-Produce Family Films'. *The Economic Times*, 19 May 2011, unpaginated.

Wasko, Janet. *Understanding Disney: The Manufacture of Fantasy* (Cambridge and Malden: Polity, 2001).

Watts, Steven. *The Magic Kingdom: Walt Disney and the American Way of Life* (Columbia: University of Missouri Press, 1997).

Weinraub, Bernard, 'Fun for the Family Is No Longer "Pollyanna"', *The New York Times*, 22 July 1997, p. C9.

Wells, Paul. *Understanding Animation* (London and New York: Routledge, 1998).

Wells, Paul. *Animation and America* (Edinburgh: Edinburgh University Press, 2002).

'What the Picture Did for Me'. *Motion Picture Herald*, 23 September 1939, p. 60.

'What the Picture Did for Me'. *Motion Picture Herald*, 21 October 1939, p. 55.

'What the Picture Did for Me'. *Motion Picture Herald*, 4 November 1939, p. 58.

'What the Picture Did for Me'. *Motion Picture Herald*, 23 December 1939, p. 51.

'What the Picture Did for Me'. *Motion Picture Herald*, 30 December 1939, p. 57.

'What the Picture Did for Me'. *Motion Picture Herald*, 20 January 1940, p. 58.

Wheare, K. C. *Report of the Committee on Children and the Cinema* (London: H. M. Stationary Office, 1950).

Willig, Caren. 'The Zeitgeist of Emil und die Detektive'. *Emil and the Detectives* DVD (BFI, 2013), pp. 5–7.

Wilson, Justin. 'Producer Radnitz Makes "Family Pictures" His Way'. *The Cavalier Daily*, 3 February 1994, p. 7.

The Wizard of Oz press book (BFI).

Wojcik-Andrews, Ian. *Children's Films: History, Ideology, Pedagogy, Theory* (New York: Garland, 2000).

Wood, Robin. *Hollywood from Vietnam to Reagan* (New York: Columbia University Press, 1986).

Zipes, Jack. 'Once Upon a Time Beyond Disney: Contemporary Fairy-Tale Films for Children' in Cary Bazalgette and David Buckingham (eds), *In Front of the Children: Screen Entertainment and Young Audiences* (London: British Film Institute, 1995), pp. 109–26.

Zipes, Jack. *The Enchanted Screen: The Unknown History of Fairy-Tale Films* (New York: Routledge, 2011).

Zipes, Jack, Pauline Greenhill, and Kendra Magnus-Johnston (eds), *Fairy-Tale Films Beyond Disney: International Perspectives* (London and New York: Routledge, 2016).

INDEX